D0958414

ACCEPT NOTHING LESS

Other Resources by
Jim Burns

Confident Parenting

Confident Parenting DVD Kit

Creating an Intimate Marriage

Creating an Intimate Marriage Audiobook

Creating an Intimate Marriage DVD Kit

The Purity Code

The Purity Code Audio Resource

Teaching Your Children Healthy Sexuality

*Teaching Your Children Healthy Sexuality
Parent/Child Combo Pack*

Teaching Your Children Healthy Sexuality DVD Kit

JIM BURNS

ACCEPT NOTHING LESS

GOD'S BEST FOR YOUR BODY, MIND, AND HEART

BETHANYHOUSE
MINNEAPOLIS, MINNESOTA

Accept Nothing Less
Copyright © 1991, 1995, 2008
Jim Burns

Newly edited and updated.

Previously published as *Radical Respect*, Harvest House Publishers, 1991, and *Radical Love*, Regal Books, 1995.

Cover design by Lookout Design, Inc.

Published by Bethany House Publishers
11400 Hampshire Avenue South
Bloomington, Minnesota 55438

Bethany House Publishers is a division of
Baker Publishing Group, Grand Rapids, Michigan.

Printed in the United States of America

In keeping with biblical principles of creation stewardship, Baker Publishing Group advocates the responsible use of our natural resources. As a member of the Green Press Initiative, our company uses recycled paper when possible. The text paper of this book is comprised of 30% post-consumer waste.

green press INITIATIVE

Library of Congress Cataloging-in-Publication Data

Burns, Jim, 1953-
   Accept nothing less : God's best for your body, mind, and heart / Jim Burns.
       p.   cm. — (Pure foundations)
   Previously published as : Radical respect, 1991 and Radical love, 1995.
   Summary: "Youth and family authority Jim Burns speaks to teens on sex and relationships. Presents biblical values about honoring God with the body, mind, and heart"—Provided by publisher.
       ISBN 978-0-7642-0212-4 (pbk. : alk. paper)   1. Teenagers—Sexual behavior—Juvenile literature. 2. Sex—Religious aspects—Juvenile literature. I. Title.

   HQ27.B87   2008
   241'.66—dc22

                                                                2008028762

To
Doug Webster and Doug Fields,
friends and co-workers
who by your zeal for life and ministry
challenge me to keep my priorities straight.

Special thanks to
Cathy
for your constant support
and ministry of "lending" me to others.

Wayne Rice
for planting the seed
to write on this subject so many years ago.

Donna Toberty, Karen Walters, Jill Corey, Carrie Steele, Judy
Hedgren, and Cindy Ward for your incredible help through these years
of writing and speaking on this subject.

The Bethany crowd: Kyle Duncan, Jeff Braun, Natasha Sperling, and
so many other wonderful people at Bethany House Publishers

JIM BURNS, PhD, founded the ministry of HomeWord in 1985 with the goal of bringing help and hope to struggling families. As host of the radio broadcast *HomeWord With Jim Burns*, which is heard daily in over eight hundred communities, Jim's passion is to build God-honoring families through communicating practical truths that will enable adults and young people alike to live out their Christian faith.

In addition to the radio program, Jim speaks to thousands around the world each year through seminars and conferences. He is an award-winning author whose books include *The Purity Code, Teaching Your Children Healthy Sexuality*, and *Confident Parenting*.

Jim and his wife, Cathy, and their three daughters and son-in-law live in Southern California.

Contents

> > > > > > > > > > > > > > >
< < < < < < < < < < <

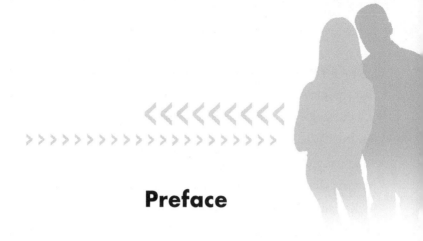

Preface

Three events in recent years have had a huge influence on my life. One was a rally in Fresno, California; one was at the foot of our nation's Capitol; the other was at a high school in Mission Viejo, California.

Fresno, California

The night before the Fresno rally to promote sexual purity, I spoke to 350 somewhat desperate and frightened but enthusiastic parents about how to talk to their kids about sex. That night, I asked how many of them had talked about sex with their parents from a positive, value-centered perspective when they were younger. Exactly twelve hands were raised. A vast majority of the parents had received absolutely no sex education from home, and a few apparently had received negative information.

One man said, "On my sixteenth birthday, my mom gave me a set of keys to our car and my dad threw a condom at me and said, 'You'll need this along with the car keys.' "

The next night, more than two thousand students jammed into an auditorium that supposedly seated fourteen hundred people. It was a fire marshal's nightmare. I challenged the students to make a commitment to sexual purity, to live by something called the Purity Code. It's a kind of experience that goes against the grain of today's culture. When I was finished, I invited them to respond by signing a sexual purity pledge card and bringing it to the front. I watched students literally run forward, and when they would see a friend who had made the same courageous decision and commitment to the Purity Code, they would hug or high-five each other. We now had more than fifteen hundred students crammed into the front of the auditorium, singing and celebrating the huge pile of sexual purity pledge cards on the steps of the stage. Seeing those students respond to a positive, healthy view of sexuality was wonderful.

A reporter from Fox News interviewed me that night and asked, "You mean there are still teenagers who actually are excited about sexual purity?"

I said, "Everybody isn't doing 'it,' and these students will carry a lot less baggage into their marriages because of their courageous decisions."

I've met thousands of students who have deeply regretted some of the sexually promiscuous decisions in their lives, but I still haven't met a person who chose to wait until marriage and regretted that decision.

Washington, D.C.

The event was held in front of our nation's Capitol. Over two hundred thousand sexual purity pledge cards, signed by young people throughout the country, had been placed on the lawn in front of the Capitol. That evening, some thirty-five thousand people gathered to have a prayer rally and to celebrate the positive decision of almost a quarter of a million students who were standing for a biblical call to sexual purity.

As I walked along the National Mall and looked out over the crowd and all those cards, I realized once again that in the midst of a scary culture, a large group of young people are making wholesome decisions. That night, I was overwhelmed with the fact that your generation does have hope.

Capistrano Valley High School, Mission Viejo, California

I stood in front of twenty-four students in Mr. Leander's first-period psychology class. The topic of discussion was sexual abstinence and AIDS. The students listened attentively and the conversation was excellent. Then I played a game called "To Take a Stand." Basically, I would make a statement, and the students could agree or disagree with the statement; then we would discuss their opinions.

Here was my statement: "It is a wise decision to wait until marriage to have sexual intercourse." They voted. Not one student agreed with the statement. *Zero!* I walked back into my office that day somewhat discouraged, yet more motivated than ever to offer students like you the truth that you *can* choose to live by the Purity Code and *accept nothing less* than God's best for your body, mind, eyes, and heart. The cost is high and you will probably be in the minority of your friends, but with self-discipline and God's help, you can be spared much heartbreak. In today's world, that may mean the difference between life and death.

The "Straight Scoop"

I was speaking at an all-day event for high-school students in North Carolina. It was one of those awesome times when I could tell we were really connecting. I told the twenty-five hundred students that the average sixteen-year-old guy has a sexual thought every twenty seconds. They laughed and pointed to all the sixteen-year-olds who were now ducking under their seats. At the break, a good-looking guy wearing a letterman's jacket came up to me and said, "Hi, Jim. I'm Ryan and I'm sixteen."

"Nice to meet you," I responded. "What's up?"

"You know that statistic about having a sexual thought every twenty seconds?" I nodded my head, and he continued. "Well, what am I supposed to think about the other nineteen seconds? It's *always* on my mind!" We laughed, but he was serious.

Sex and dating are often on the minds of young people (and older people too!). I believe you deserve the "straight scoop" when it comes to discussing sexuality. I've had the privilege of talking with and listening to students about their sexuality my entire adult life, and they've taught me a lot. They've taught me, for instance, that they are mature enough to handle discussing even the most sensitive issues. They have been willing to be open, honest, and often quite blunt when they ask questions or offer their opinions. They have also trusted me with accounts of their own experiences and lessons they learned the hard way. (Because we all can learn from these real-life situations, I've changed my young friends' names and included some of their stories here.)

Overall, I'm guessing that you're a lot like the students I know. You truly desire to be all that God wants you to be. You want a Christian perspective on the issues you face every day. I'm afraid, though, that too many students have an incredibly warped idea of God's view of sexuality. I find myself saying again and again that God is not a grinch when it comes to sex. He created sex, He sees it as very good, and because He loves you, He wants the very best for you. He wants you to *accept nothing less.*

An outgrowth of this dialogue with hundreds of students is this book. The problem is, you receive all kinds of mixed messages these days when it comes to sex. The secular world assumes everybody is having sex, and the Christian world—both parents and the church—is often far too quiet. Kids today are making unhealthy sexual decisions based on:

- Peer influence;
- Emotional involvement that exceeds their maturity level; and
- Lack of positive, value-centered sex education.

Studies tell us that the more positive, healthy, value-centered sex education kids receive, the less promiscuous they will become.

This book is my attempt to give you and other students healthy, straightforward Christian information on relationships and sex. May it challenge, inspire, and educate you to be all God desires you to be.

Accept Nothing Less,

Jim Burns
Dana Point, California

How to Use This Book

Thank you so much for picking up this book. It is part of the PURE FOUNDATIONS series, which includes age-appropriate books and other resources on how students can honor God with their bodies, minds, eyes, and hearts. I see *Accept Nothing Less* as a conversation with guys and girls in their mid- to upper-teens. It builds on the information presented in *The Purity Code*, which is for younger teens, but it's not necessary to read that book first. *Accept Nothing Less* covers a lot of ground in its twenty-three brief chapters, and compared with the other books, it includes more discussion ideas and curriculum-type exercises (not anything like regular homework, though!). In a perfect world, this book would be read together with parents. I realize some students will read it on their own and others will work through the pages in their youth group or in school. However, whenever possible, a parent is the best person to teach his or her child about healthy, value-centered sexuality and relationships.

Over the many years I have spoken about this subject, I have been incredibly blessed by how open students are to this message. Not everyone is making unwise decisions!

My hope is that *Accept Nothing Less* will be much more than just another book on sexuality. It is a learning experience. For one thing, it doesn't just focus on staying pure before marriage. Sexual integrity should start at a young age and then extend throughout our lifetime. It affects our self-image, how we treat members of the opposite sex, and how we view and enjoy intimacy in marriage, as well as how firm we are in keeping faithful in mind and body. Although it's a great book to read alone, it's also written with groups in mind. It is based on the idea that students learn best when *they* talk, not just leaders or parents.

Included at the end of each chapter you'll find three sections. *Things to Think About* provides general questions that will help clarify the issues presented in the chapter. *Respect Builders* asks students to make personal decisions or take practical action steps that affect the way they view themselves and others. *Team Effort* ties everything together with group exercises and discussion activities that allow teens to talk over their feelings with each other and with trusted adults such as parents and youth workers. The emphasis is on:

- Discussion and interaction;
- Goal setting and decision making;
- Thinking critically about important issues;
- Relating with peers and adults.

Accept Nothing Less is designed for a variety of uses:

- *Small group discussion and interaction*—Youth groups can use *Accept Nothing Less* as a helpful and lively interacting tool.
- *Retreat and camp format*—More positive sex education can often take place outside the classroom in a non-threatening environment.

- *Church school and youth group curriculum*—These subjects and chapters have been time-tested to relate to where kids are today.
- *Christian school classes*—This is an excellent resource for classes on health and sex education.

Chapter One

The Story of Taylor and Lindsay

When I first met Lindsay, I knew she would be a real asset to our youth group. She was enthusiastic and fun loving, and when it came to talking seriously about our faith in Christ, she could settle down and really dig in to the Scriptures. What a joy to be around her! Now, two-and-a-half years later, Lindsay sat in my office and sobbed uncontrollably. Her story went something like this . . .

Although she had dated in high school, she had never really been serious with anyone until Taylor came along. Taylor was in the leadership core at church. He was popular at school and active in student government, and he was a real gentleman. At first, most of their dates were double dates or church functions. Very quickly they fell head over heels for each other. For Lindsay, life began to revolve around Taylor and the time they spent together.

A few weeks turned into a few months, and the "perfect couple" began to seem more and more inseparable. After youth group, instead of going out for a bite to eat with the rest of the crew, they would make an excuse and end up spending an hour or so kissing in Taylor's car. They both had high moral standards, but they were so much in love that in the next few months they found themselves slipping, in Lindsay's words, "from light kissing to heavy kissing to making out to just about everything but sex." At this point Lindsay was what some call a "technical virgin." They would do everything but . . . go all the way. Slowly but surely their dates had changed from doing fun and active things with a group of friends to situations in which they could be physically close. Almost every date was filled with very heavy make-out sessions.

Sometimes Taylor and Lindsay would talk about their relationship. Although they were both in high school and wanted to attend college, marriage was a possibility. Now, however, both Lindsay and Taylor felt guilty about their physical relationship. They tried to talk about it, but it was a difficult subject to discuss. Although they both tried to stop being so physical, it was getting harder to stop. They found themselves communicating less and less verbally and more and more sexually.

The Lindsay who now sat in my office was a serious young woman struggling with guilt and confusion. It was difficult for her to share her experiences. She and Taylor had been, in her words, "doing it" for about two months. The night before, though, Taylor had opened up to her and shared his true inner feelings. He loved her, but he felt tremendous guilt about their physical relationship; school was going badly; and he wanted to be more involved with church. Although he loved Lindsay, he thought that it was best to break up.

Lindsay was crushed, yet she knew that most of what Taylor was saying was true. She came to my office looking for answers. She still wanted to be with Taylor, and she desperately wanted to know how to overcome sexual temptation. In her Bible, Lindsay had found a verse that she believed to be true, but she didn't quite know how to apply it. It says: "No temptation has overtaken you that is not common to man. God is faithful, and he will not let you be tempted beyond your strength, but with the temptation will also provide the way of escape, that you may be able to endure it" (1 Corinthians 10:13 RSV).

Lindsay believed that God is faithful, and she recognized that her temptation was common to others. Her problem was trying to figure out a way to escape her temptation and remain true to her convictions. We continued to talk for some time and came up with the following:

Six Positive Guidelines for Overcoming Sexual Temptation

Talk About the Problem With Your Girlfriend or Boyfriend

Some of you haven't dated or experienced sexual temptations yet, but when you do, it's important to know what to expect. For one thing, if you don't feel comfortable talking to a boyfriend or girlfriend about your physical relationship, yet you continue to go further than you think is right, then you have a problem. A good relationship includes open communication; in a good relationship, the guy and girl should be willing and able to talk about the problem. When Lindsay finally did talk with Taylor, she found out that he had the same guilty feelings she did. Incidentally, when you decide to talk with your girlfriend or boyfriend about your sexual temptation and struggles, try having that conversation over ice cream or walking home from school, not where you usually go to be alone together or right after you've slipped.

Set Standards

The best advice our premarital counselor gave to my wife, Cathy, and I was to set standards *before* becoming swept up in the heat of emotions. Set standards that are right for both individuals involved. Again, take advantage of casual hangout time to talk about your physical relationship and decide what your limits will be. Then when temptation comes your way, it will be easier not to violate your conscious decisions. First, make the standard on your own and then talk about it. If I might be perfectly blunt, set the standards that you believe God would want you to set. Get help from understanding parents, your church youth worker, or another God-honoring person. No one ever regretted having extremely conservative standards. Millions of students now regret having lax standards.

Plan Dates That Will Be Fun and Social

When Joseph was tempted to have an affair with Potiphar's wife, he ran out of the house to flee temptation. He didn't even take time to pick up his coat! (See Genesis 39:2–15.) One of the best ways to avoid sexual temptation is to stay away from places where it is easy to be tempted. Plan dates that are fun and social. Double dates, for instance, can often be more fun than "single" dates. Also, in a recent poll of high-school students, an overwhelming 92 percent said they would rather go on a "creative cheap date" than on an "expensive romantic date." Plan your dates in advance and keep away from secluded parking spots and dark roads!

Pray Together

If you are a Christian, I hope you will want to go out with other Christians. A great way to grow in your faith and develop a better relationship with your boyfriend or girlfriend is to pray together. Praying together draws you closer to God and to each other. Praying together helps you set proper priorities for your relationship. And, naturally, praying together as a couple will help both of you resist sexual temptation.

Break Up

One of the hardest things to do is to break off a relationship. It's perfectly normal to become dependent on a dating partner and wonder if anyone else will ever go out with us. There is no easy way to break off a relationship, especially one in which you have been sexually active. Yet many times the very best thing for both people would be to break up. If your relationship was meant to be, you can always get back together later on when you've both become more mature.

Allow God to Be a Part of Your Dating Relationship

People of all ages can struggle to allow God to take an active part in certain areas of their lives. This is certainly true when it comes to sexuality. For some reason, it is difficult to give God this area of life. I think sometimes we're afraid God will take all the fun out of it.

If it's true (and I believe it is) that God cares about every area of our lives, then He definitely cares about our sexuality and wants the best for us. If you, as a Christian, allow God to take an active role in your dating life, you'll find it easier to flee temptation.

Epilogue

Taylor and Lindsay decided to break up. (It wasn't easy!) Here is what happened. After Lindsay and I met that day, Taylor and Lindsay came over to our home that night and talked with Cathy and me. They decided to give the relationship one more try. This time they created boundaries and set standards that were much more conservative and in line with Scripture. We prayed together, and they decided that if they broke those standards they would have to break up. One week later, they broke the standards and then broke off the relationship.

The story didn't end there, however. A few years ago I was officiating at a wedding that both Taylor and Lindsay were attending. When the ceremony was over, I was talking with several young adults from the youth group the bride and groom belonged to, when Lindsay came up to me and asked if we could talk privately. "Sure, Lindsay, what's up?" She had tears in her eyes and said, "Don't get me wrong. I am doing okay, but I feel *paralyzed* from my relationship with Taylor from years ago. It affects the way I do relationships today!" We talked and decided to get together to talk again.

Minutes later Taylor came up to me. I hadn't seen him since high school. He'd been away at a college on the other side of the country. He said, "I saw you talking with Lindsay a moment ago. How is she doing?" I wasn't the one to tell him anything, so I just said, "Fine, why do you ask?" His eyes moistened up (us guys have a hard time saying we cried!), and he said, "Don't get me wrong. I'm doing okay, but I feel *paralyzed* from my experience with Lindsay so many years ago." I wanted to shout, "I've heard those words before!"

Taylor and Lindsay felt paralyzed from their past relationship. They would need to move on. They would need to change the way they did relationships. They would need to realize this truth: *The decisions you make today about your sexuality and relationships can play a determining factor in how you carry out your life.*

Things to Think About

1. Have you known people who were in a situation similar to Taylor and Lindsay's? How did it work out?
2. What do you think Corinthians 10:13 has to say about sexual temptation?
3. How do you feel about the suggestion to pray together to help overcome temptation?
4. What do you think it means to allow God to become a part of a dating relationship? What are some practical ways in which a couple can include the Lord in their times together?

Respect Builders

1. Set standards. Have you consciously thought through your standards for dating behavior? If you have, write your standards on a piece of paper. If you haven't, think about it now and write down some of your ideas. Seek the advice of God-honoring people.

2. Allow God to be part of your dating relationship. How alive is your relationship with God right now? Check yourself on the chart that follows.

Action	Never	Once in a while	Once a month	Once a week	Almost every day
I read the Bible					
I pray					
I attend worship services					
I do fun things with other Christians					
I talk about Jesus with Christian friends					
I talk about Jesus with friends who don't know Him					
I ask for God's help rather than trying to handle problems myself					
I try to include God in my relationship with the opposite sex					

You cannot keep your dating life separate from the rest of your life. If you are active and growing in your relationship with God, He can help you with your dating relationships. If you come to Him only occasionally or only in an emergency, you are missing out on a lot that He can do for you.

Team Effort

Have one person read the story of Taylor and Lindsay to the group. Discuss the question: What would you have said to Lindsay or Taylor if one of them had come to you with this problem? List several ideas on the board or on a piece of paper.

If you want some help in setting your standards, check the Scriptures listed below. Remember that these are not specific rules. Instead, they are principles you can use as guides in determining what you will do. Write down what these verses teach. Use your own words.

1 Corinthians 3:16
1 Corinthians 6:18–20
1 Corinthians 13:1–7
Ephesians 5:1–2

Chapter Two

How Far Is Too Far?

I wish I had a dollar for every time I have been asked, "How far is too far?" or "Are we allowed to make out?" or "What does the Bible say about oral sex?" I'd be a rich man! This, of course, is one of the big issues we must face when dealing with our sexuality. Sometimes I wish the Bible were more specific when it comes to this subject. But it's not. (Believe me, as a teenager I thumbed through the pages of the Bible looking for answers myself!)

The problem lies, I think, in the fact that most people ask the wrong questions. We shouldn't ask, "How far *can* I go?" Instead the question is, "How far *should* I go?" The issue is not, "Am I allowed to make out?" but rather "Should I make out?" People today are often looking for black-and-white answers. When it comes to the subject of making out, however, answers aren't easy and there seems to be a gray area.

First, let's define "making out." A discussion of the evolution of terms can make for a funny conversation. In my day, we called strong kissing and fondling of the breast and sexual organs "petting." Today I would be laughed off stage if I used the term "petting," right? "Making out" probably isn't the best phrase either because, again, in my generation, "making out" meant heavy kissing. Today, for many people, making out is more than heavy kissing. Making out is a combination of kissing (a lot) and touching, caressing, or fondling intimate parts of another person's body. There is no manual that says French kissing is okay but fondling the breasts is not okay. In fact, there is no manual to even say what making out is and what it is not. So for the time being, let's keep it as simple as the definition in this paragraph.

Perhaps a more important question than "What is making out?" is "Why make out?" This is where we might get some real insight. In his book *How Far Can I Go?* Larry Richards says, "Biologically, [making out] isn't designed to *satisfy* our emotions, but to *stimulate* and *excite* us, and lead to the fullest expression of sex in marriage" (emphasis added).[1]

He's right. Making out and arousal (arousal means experiencing sexual excitement) at times can be synonymous. Making out leads toward the ultimate sexual satisfaction—intercourse. God is very clear that sexual intercourse outside of marriage is not what He believes is best for you. Now don't get me wrong. I don't think that every couple who has ever made out will have intercourse. It is important, however, to understand that making out is not designed to satisfy our emotions or our physical desires. Instead, it does the exact opposite by stimulating and exciting those emotions and desires, making it even more difficult to stop.

Something else to think about is that too many times, making out is focused simply on personal pleasure and not on the other person. Some people in a highly sexualized relationship lose sight of their boyfriend or girlfriend as they try to stimulate and satisfy their own sexual desires. Making out can become a self-centered experience rather than an effort to communicate love for another person.

The other important thing to mention about making out is the scientific fact that this kind of sexual stimulation is similar to taking certain drugs: It often takes more and more to satisfy. I've spent time with too many couples who have started their physical relationships innocently, but because of the strong drive toward sexual fulfillment in intercourse, they have found themselves guilt-ridden, pregnant, or facing a broken relationship. Young people must realize that within every normal human being there is a built-in sex drive. We thank God for it, yet we also must control it. And with God's help, we *can* control it. Whom we place in the driver's seat can make all the difference when it comes to our sexual experiences.

Because our sexuality is so important to us, we need to count the cost before we become physically intimate. I think about Jessica as I write that sentence. Jessica was a lonely girl in my youth group. She started dating one of the popular guys at her school, and, in her words, "fell madly and passionately in love with him." After they broke up, she slipped into my office one day, crying uncontrollably: "I'm so freaking mad. I feel so cheap . . . I have high standards and now I don't even like him! How could I have given so much of my body to someone I thought I liked but now can't stand? I just didn't think about how much I could lose!"

That's real insight for a sixteen-year-old. Unfortunately, Jessica learned the hard way that her sexuality was uniquely personal and that if she gave herself freely before marriage she would probably regret it later. I hope others will not have to go through the pain Jessica experienced to figure out what she learned.

In this chapter, I have tried not to use scare tactics. All I want to do is give you some facts to think about. Making out, having oral sex, and doing other sexual acts on the fringe of intercourse is serious business. Technical virginity is being discussed on campus and on MTV as if it is a great new idea. Someone once said, "Everything *but* . . . leads to going all the way." I'm not writing for the sexually promiscuous student who is willing to settle for second best in life. I'm writing for the person who is curious about sexuality and yet wants to be all that God wants him or her to be, and who wants to accept nothing less than God's best for them. Having discussed some of the problem areas, now let's look at some of the answers.

Unfortunately, there are no easy answers. Most of the Christian books on youth and sexuality simply say, "Don't have sex until marriage." If people followed this advice, they would save themselves a lot of heartache and sorrow. Consider for a moment that the average person falls in love three to five times before marriage.[2] If heavy make-out sessions—or more—are part of each relationship, there will surely be some confusion as well as pain and guilt when it comes to sexuality. This is not to mention the fact that premarital sexual relationships do tend to bring "baggage" into your eventual marriage relationship.

My answer is not as simple as "don't do it." It is very possible that you may have an intense make-out experience before marriage. What I want to do, however, is to save you as much grief and confusion as possible. As I said earlier, the Bible is silent on the subject of making out. Throughout the Scriptures, though, we see clearly God's desire that sexual intercourse be saved for your marriage partner. But what about all the other actions, from light kissing to oral sex?

I think an important question to ask is "What would be pleasing to God in our relationship?" When we begin to view our relationships with this question in mind, we begin to look at our sexuality from a positive perspective rather than a negative one.

For several years, I've given students an exercise in setting standards for themselves. It's an exercise that will help you set standards before you reach Inspiration Point (or whatever you call the local kissing hangout) and find it more difficult to handle your hormones. I'm always amazed at the maturity I see as students consider the question, "How far should I go?"

It is important to think about this issue and to develop guidelines for a physical relationship even before a relationship develops. Never try to set standards in the midst of passion. Instead, thoughtfully establish the standards for your physical relationship that you feel would best glorify God. Remember that your body is the temple of the Holy Spirit (see 1 Corinthians 6:19). Also think about what would be best for your relationship with your boyfriend or girlfriend. I think you'll agree in the long run that what is best for God will definitely be best for you.

Most people will probably kiss before marriage. However, my friend Dennis Rainey of Family Life Today shared a video with me of his son's wedding. The first time he kissed his bride was on their wedding day. Dennis and I laughed together as he said they kissed during the ceremony, kissed going down the aisle, they kissed in the back of the church, and they kissed often through the reception. The beauty and innocence of that incredible show of discipline is wonderful. I'm not suggesting that is the norm. I am saying that the less involved in premarital sexuality, the healthier the marriage relationship can be from the beginning.

Things to Think About

1. In your own words, how would you define "making out"?
2. Why do people have such a difficult time setting standards for their sexual behavior?
3. Do you think guys or girls are more interested in sex? Or do you think both have about the same interest?
4. How do you feel about this statement: A person who is heavily making out tends to lose sight of the partner, focusing rather on his or her own pleasure.
5. If your boyfriend's or girlfriend's standards are different from yours, how will these differences affect your ability to maintain a relationship that is comfortable and healthy for both of you?

Respect Builders

1. Set standards before Inspiration Point. (This Respect Builder goes a step further than number 1 in the first chapter.)

   The following chart gives you an opportunity to think about specific actions and to determine the type of relationship in which each one belongs. Also, consider these actions in light of this question: "What would be pleasing to God?" And remember that God isn't out to make your life miserable.

   Before you begin to work on the chart, note that the headings range from "Friendship" to "Marriage." At the bottom is a list of abbreviations; each letter stands for a certain action. Write each letter in the column or columns representing the relationship in which you think the action would be pleasing to God. For example, "SI" for "sexual intercourse" has already been placed in the "Marriage" column. We know God's will for intercourse; it is clearly set forth in the Bible. For the other actions listed, thoughtfully and logically determine the standards that will best please and glorify God.

How Far Should I Go?

Friendship	Dating	Steady	Engage-ment	Marriage
				SI

L = Looking	h = Holding hands
H = Holding hands constantly	HH = Hugging
k = Light kissing	K = Heavy kissing
F = French kissing	B = Fondling the breasts
SO = Fondling the sexual organs/oral sex	SI = Sexual intercourse

2. If you are in a dating relationship right now, you might want to ask your girlfriend or boyfriend to complete the chart too. Then you could compare answers and discuss any differences you find. Just be sure you do this when both of you are calm and rational—not in the heat of emotions!

Team Effort

A debate:

To explore the pros and cons of making out, cluster students into two or more groups of five or six members each. Assign half of the groups to the "pro" side and the other half to the "con" side. Suggest that all students read 1 Corinthians 3:16; 6:9–20; and 10:31–11:1 as they formulate their arguments. (Some may find that they disagree with the position assigned to them. In that case, as in a school debate, they should simply come up with the best arguments they can—even if they do not agree with them.) After allowing some time for preparation, let the proponents of each position state their cases. After each group makes an initial statement, allow time for fuller discussion of the issue.

Chapter Three

Why Wait?

Lauren and Josh made an appointment to see me in my office. Although I barely knew them, I did know they had been dating for some time. They walked into my office, sat down, and got right to the point. Josh started the conversation by saying, "Last week Lauren and I had sex for the first time. It brought us even closer together. We love each other a lot, and . . . well . . . we're planning to get married in a few years, and we want to know why we should wait until we're married to have sex!"

I asked Lauren what she thought. I think she was a little stunned that Josh had opened up so quickly, but she nodded her head to indicate that she had the same question. But Lauren had a few more reservations about premarital sex than Josh did. She explained, "Afterward, I did feel really close to Josh, but I've been dealing with a lot of guilt since then. And I'm afraid I might get pregnant or something!"

I really liked Josh and Lauren. I appreciated their openness and their desire to make the right decision. We talked for two hours, and during those two hours they shared more of their dreams and doubts. Yes, they did love each other, but both thought they were too young to seriously consider marriage. The conversation also revealed that Josh was much more interested in having sex than Lauren was.

When they left the office, I believed I'd made two new friends. They wanted to see me again, but both of them would be away from our town for a total of six weeks for various reasons. Lauren asked if I would think about why they should wait, write them a letter listing the reasons, and then send copies to both of them to think about and discuss together when they returned. That was a unique request, but I said I would try. We exchanged e-mail addresses and hugged each other, I prayed for them, and we said good-bye for six weeks. Here's the letter I wrote to them:

Dear Josh and Lauren:

You are two very special people. I think God has great things in store for both of you. I appreciate your willingness to be all that God desires you to be. Our time together on Friday has really made me do some heavy thinking and even some extra reading on what you called "the big drama."

Let me preface what I'm going to say by reminding you of what I said on Friday. I realize that many well-meaning people make the mistake of "going all the way" before marriage. Although the Bible is clear on the subject of intercourse outside of marriage, God is merciful and patient and He loves us unconditionally. I can also understand how the normal sex drives of two healthy people who love each other can cause an intense desire for sex. However, I'm even more convinced than before that it is God's desire for people to refrain from premarital intercourse. In my opinion, it is always the right thing to do when you obey the instructions of God by following the Purity Code so that you can have the very best God has in store for you concerning relationships.

I came across this quote this past weekend. It's from *The Screwtape Letters* by C. S. Lewis: "The truth is that whenever a man lies with a woman, there, whether they like it or not, a transcendental relation is set up between them which must either be eternally enjoyed or eternally endured."[1] I can't think of anything more intimate or personal than sharing each other's bodies, emotions, and spirits in sexual union. That's why I'm so concerned about today's promiscuous sex. It's the philosophy of "easy come, easy go" or "if it feels good, do it." I know you agree with me that sex outside of marriage greatly cheapens intimacy. I know this is not your intention, but I still have some huge reservations even though you two love each other.

I've made up some questions that I hope you will discuss together. They may help you thoughtfully and carefully arrive at a decision to wait or not to wait. Keep in mind that I write these questions with the sense that you are both Christians who truly desire to grow in your Christian faith.

1. Will premarital sex lessen the meaning of intercourse in marriage for either of you?
2. Does your conscience make you feel uneasy during or after sex? Could this be the Holy Spirit challenging you?
3. Are you both equally committed to each other?
4. Are you totally convinced in your hearts that the other person is "the one" forever?
5. What do you believe the Bible has to say about premarital sex? Here are a few verses to look at: Acts 15:20; 1 Corinthians 6:13, 18–20; Ephesians 5:3; 1 Thessalonians 4:1–8; and 1 Peter 2:11.

6. You both seem to desire God's best for you. Will having sex affect your usefulness to God or your relationship with Him?

7. Will having sex before marriage damage in any way your relationship with each other?

8. Could premarital intercourse damage your communication or result in either a loss of respect for or mistrust of each other?

9. Will premarital sex help, hinder, or not affect your spiritual relationship to each other?

10. Have you thought through birth control methods and the possibilities of parenthood and marriage because of pregnancy?

11. What are your motives for having sex? Are they pure?

I'm convinced that any couple contemplating premarital sex should take a look at these questions and deal with them honestly.

I also want to include a list of statements for you to ponder. I found this list in an excellent book called *Sex, Love, or Infatuation: How Can I Really Know?* by Ray Short. In the chapter "To Be or Not to Be a Virgin," Ray writes that "science has established nine facts concerning the probable effect of premarital sex on your marriage."[2] I will list them for you. I wish I could include the whole chapter, but I'll simply list the statements. When you get together, you can discuss them as a couple. This will be a good exercise in communication and a great chance to learn a lot about premarital sex.

Fact 1: Premarital sex tends to break up couples.

Fact 2: Many men do not want to marry a woman who has had intercourse with someone else. (This fact can be said for many young women as well.)

Fact 3: Those who have premarital sex tend to have less happy marriages.

Fact 4: Those who have premarital sex are more likely to have their marriage end in divorce.

Fact 5: Persons and couples who have had premarital sex are more likely to have extramarital affairs as well.

Fact 6: Having premarital sex may fool you into marrying a person who is not right for you.

Fact 7: Persons and couples with premarital sex experience seem to achieve sexual satisfaction sooner after they are married. HOWEVER—

Fact 8: They are likely to be less satisfied overall with their sex life during marriage.

Fact 9: Poor premarital sexual habits can be carried over to spoil sex in marriage.[3]

Each fact is worth your discussing. He has really made some important points for you to consider carefully.

The more I think about it, the more I respect you both for taking the time to consider what is best for you, for your relationship to each other, and for your relationship with God. I'm afraid too many couples simply move into sex too quickly. Without having given it much thought at all, they create a situation that can seriously impact their entire lives.

One last thing before I conclude. Even though right now you have little doubt that you probably will get married, let me play devil's advocate for a moment. A relationship authority once said, "One study shows an average of five 'real loves' for kids between ninth grade and the second year of college."[4] You've both said that you have a long way to go before marriage. What if you don't get married? I know that I was thoroughly convinced I was going to marry Geri in junior high, Nancy in tenth grade, and Carol in twelfth grade—it's amazing how our minds can change!

I realize that I've given you a lot to think about. I believe in you both and look forward to spending more time together in the future. Thank you for the real privilege of being included in your lives.

Blessings,

Jim

Things to Think About

1. Do you think Josh and Lauren made the right decision to discuss their dilemma with a counselor? Why or why not?

2. What stands out in your mind from my letter as being good advice?

3. Which of the eleven questions that I asked Josh and Lauren were the most significant?

4. What did you think of the nine "facts" I shared? Do you agree or disagree with them? Why?

5. One study has shown that the average person has five "real loves" between ninth grade and the second year of college. Of course, this is a general statement, but how does this statistic affect your opinion of teen marriages?

Take some time to respond to the questions I asked Lauren and Josh. If your situation is not the same as theirs, answer as you think you would answer if you were in their shoes.

1. Will premarital sex lessen the meaning of intercourse in marriage for either of you?

2. Does (or would) your conscience make you feel uneasy during or after sexual intercourse?
3. Are you both equally committed to each other?
4. Are you totally convinced in your hearts that the other person is "the one" forever?
5. What do you believe the Bible has to say about premarital sex? Here are a few verses to ponder: Acts 15:20; 1 Corinthians 6:13, 18–20; Ephesians 5:3; 1 Thessalonians 4:1–8; and 1 Peter 2:11.
6. Will having sex before marriage damage in any way your relationship with each other?
7. Could premarital sex damage your communication? Could it cause you to lose respect for your boyfriend/girlfriend? Could it cause you to mistrust him or her?
8. Will premarital sex help, hinder, or not affect your spiritual relationship to each other?
9. Have you thought through birth control methods and the possibilities of parenthood and marriage because of a pregnancy?
10. What are your motives for having sex? Are they pure?

Team Effort

Look at the nine statements quoted from the book *Sex, Love, or Infatuation: How Can I Really Know?* by Ray Short. Discuss with each other what you consider the strongest arguments against premarital sex and why.

Chapter Four

The Purity Code

Fifteen-year-old Kaylee is one of the most beautiful girls I have ever met. Her big blue eyes and radiant smile cause every head in the room to turn toward her. Not only does she possess an outward attractiveness, but her inner beauty shines bright. (Sorry guys, I'm not giving out her phone number!) One day after I spoke in chapel at her Christian high school on one of my favorite subjects—sexual purity—Kaylee came right up to me. She had the biggest grin on her face and looked as if she was about to let me in on a secret. Instead, she put her right hand in my face and showed me a beautiful ring. I said, "It's wonderful. Who's the lucky guy?"

She laughed and said, "My dad and God."

I sat down and said, "You'd better explain."

Kaylee told me a great story: "My dad took me out on my first date. We got all dressed up and went to an extra-special restaurant. We had the greatest talk about me following what you called the Purity Code. He didn't lecture; he didn't preach at me. He was just open and honest and told me how much he hoped I would be faithful to what God wants for me. When dinner was over, he handed me a present. It was a little box, wrapped really nicely. I could tell my dad didn't wrap it by himself! Inside was this beautiful ring. My dad said with real emotion, 'Your mom and I want you to have this ring as a commitment to remain sexually pure until marriage.' He pointed out three stones. The middle stone stands for my commitment to God, the stone on the left was for my commitment to my family, and the stone on the right was for my commitment to my future husband, whoever that will be." Kaylee continued, "My first date was with my dad, but I will never forget it. It was really one of the most special moments of my life."

She went on to tell me that after the date, her dad asked if she was willing to pray with him to ask God to help her remain sexually pure. Kaylee said she was willing, and they prayed. As Kaylee talked about her dad's gift and their God-honoring conversation, the power of what she said brought tears to my eyes. When she told me that her goal is to give her ring to her husband on their wedding night, I was overwhelmed by her conviction and deep desire to trust God with her heart and her body. I remember telling Kaylee how fortunate she was to have a dad and mom who cared so much.

You may have a special experience with one of your parents such as Kaylee had with her dad (I hope you do), but the odds are probably against it. Parents aren't perfect, you know, and a lot of them don't have a clue how to talk to their kids about sex and boyfriends or girlfriends. There's a good chance that their parents never taught them. But that doesn't mean you can't take a stand and live by what I call the Purity Code. Here it is. Are you willing to make this commitment?

"In honor of God, my family, and my future spouse, I commit my life to sexual purity."

The Purity Code involves:

- Honoring God with your body
- Renewing your mind for the good
- Turning your eyes from worthless things
- Guarding your heart above all else

People who do the best at living out the Purity Code don't commit to it just to please their parents or because friends are doing it. They take the time to seriously consider the decision.

To be honest, statistics tell us that you will be in the minority if you choose to live by the Code. Unfortunately, a majority of people in the United States will have had sex before they turn nineteen. However, a commitment to sexual purity will be one of the most important decisions of your life. Here's what the Bible says:

> *Do you not know that your body is a temple of the Holy Spirit, who is in you, whom you have received from God? You are not your own; you were bought at a price. Therefore honor God with your body.* (1 Corinthians 6:19–20)

Because, as a Christian, your body is the temple of the Holy Spirit and because Christ died on a cross for you, you have every reason to honor God with your body. That means, in part, giving God your sexual purity. I have never met a man or woman who regretted their decision to wait until marriage to have sex. But I've met hundreds of men and women who *wish* they had waited because of the baggage they have carried into their marriages.

Notice that the Purity Code involves more than honoring God with your body and not participating in sexual sin. A pure mind is also important. The Bible says, "Do not conform any longer to the pattern of this world, but be transformed by the renewing of your mind. Then you will be able to test and approve what God's will is—his good, pleasing and perfect will" (Romans 12:2). Even after marriage, a person needs to tune out the "bad" in culture and tune in the "good." I challenge you and other students to spend even a few minutes a day reading a devotional or Scripture. I challenge you to listen to good music that will lift you up and keep your mind set on positive things. I challenge you to find friends who provide positive, healthy conversations.

The third part of the Purity Code is to turn your eyes from worthless things. Your eyes are a window to your soul. This truth comes from Jesus, who said, "The eye is the lamp of the body. If your eyes are good, your whole body will be full of light" (Matthew 6:22). Did you know that images of everything we see are taken and stored in the brain? And the more negative and sexually explicit stuff we see—whether accidentally or on purpose—the more it will be stuck in our minds.

The final part of the Purity Code is to guard your heart above all else. This is based on Proverbs 4:23, which says, "Guard your heart above all else, for it determines the course of your life" (NLT).

My hope is that you will not wait another moment to guard your body, mind, eyes, and heart by putting down this book and committing to the Purity Code. You won't regret this decision!

What If I've Already Blown It?

Many people reading this book have already missed the mark and at one time or another have been sexually active. They've jumped the gun and are no longer sexually pure. Here's the good news: You can become pure again in the sight of God. Once you have asked for God's forgiveness and made a commitment to sexual purity, it is as if you've never sinned. The Lord told Isaiah, "I, even I, am he who blots out your transgressions, for my own sake, and remembers your sins no more" (Isaiah 43:25). That's good news for those who fall short!

In today's world, we need every possible plan to remain sexually pure. A commitment to give God your body and honor Him and your future spouse with virginity is one of the highest forms of commitment.

Things to Think About

1. What holds people back from committing to the Purity Code?
2. Who can you talk to openly and honestly about sexual issues?
3. Read 1 Corinthians 6:19–20. How does verse 19 relate to the issue of sexual purity?
4. Why is it sometimes difficult to believe that God actually does "blot out" confessed sin?
5. After reading this chapter, what decision(s) have you made about your sexuality?

Respect Builders

1. Make a decision today to live by the Purity Code. Take a moment to pray to God and commit your sexuality to Him. Pray for:

   • strength to overcome temptation;
   • wisdom on dating relationships;

- your future husband or wife;
- a continued desire to remain sexually pure.

2. Tell your parents or a friend about your decision to remain sexually pure. Once you've made a decision, there is absolutely nothing better than telling someone and asking that person to help you remain accountable to your commitment.

Team Effort

Here's a very special personal letter from Dr. James Dobson to a fifteen-year-old named Jonathan. Jonathan and his dad had an evening out much like Kaylee and her dad had. At dinner, Jonathan's dad presented him with this letter from Dr. Dobson:

> Dear Jonathan,
>
> Your dad told me that the two of you are about to have a very important talk. I've been invited to participate in the discussion by way of a letter. I was asked to say a few things about purity—sexual purity—though I don't suppose there's much I can tell you that you haven't heard before.
>
> I'm sure your parents have taught you well. But I want to encourage you to act on what you already know. Believe me, it's worth it to save sex for marriage and keep yourself pure for the woman God wants you to spend your life with. The Lord designed it that way for good reasons. Plenty of people who disregarded His plan in that area will tell you how much they regret it.
>
> You're going to need more of this kind of encouragement in the days to come. It's one thing to know what's right. Living by it is something else. Over the next few years, you'll probably face pressure to change or compromise your values—pressure from

your friends, from advertising, from television and movies, and a hundred other sources. You may even find yourself in situations where it could be easy to yield to sexual temptation.

One of the best ways of fighting back is learning to like yourself. If you feel good about you, you'll have the confidence to take a stand—even if you're the only one! Just remember who you are and what your parents have taught you. There's real strength in knowing that God loves you and has a purpose for your life!

But if you feel inferior to others, it will be that much easier to let them press you into their mold. Don't do it! The rest of your life is ahead of you, and it's worth fighting for. I hope this helps, Jonathan. I'm sure your dad will have more to say on this subject. You're a lucky guy to have parents who care about you so much! Take advantage of their wisdom and be encouraged by their love. God bless you![1]

Answer these questions:

1. What advice from this letter is the best advice for you?
2. If you could write a letter to yourself, what would you say to help keep you sexually pure?

Chapter Five

The Influence of Sexuality

One of the most powerful words in our language is that famous three-letter word: sex. Pay attention the next time you're with friends or at school—when the subject turns to sex, everyone stops to listen! One of the important questions everyone should consider is why sex has such an influence on our lives. A young friend of mine once made this comment about his own conversations: "With most of my friends, every subject we talk about gets turned into a talk about sex! It's like everyone is sex crazy!"

Well, my high-school friend was right. Our society is a little "sex crazy." I saw a T-shirt the other day that had printed in big red letters across the front, "Candy is dandy, but sex won't rot your teeth!" That's probably a true statement, but I think there is more to the whole issue than that! And to better understand our sexuality, it's important to ask ourselves why sex does have such an important influence on our lives.

The Media Appeals to Our Sexuality

Have you ever stopped to realize how frequently and effectively the media uses our sexuality to sell us products? Often you'll see a commercial on television where the most beautiful girl in the world is selling shampoo, surrounded by attractive, wealthy-looking men. Or a guy who looks like he walked out of an Abercrombie & Fitch catalog, with rippling muscles, wavy blond hair, a deep voice, and a golden tan, tries to convince you that you too can look like he does if you would simply wear a certain cologne. And what's worse is that millions of us buy that brand of shampoo or cologne because we fall for this media hype! (Believe me, it doesn't work. I've bought all that stuff and I'm still short and bald!) We are surrounded by sensual media, ranging from billboards to the latest love story at the movies. And we have to face the fact that the media will always use the power of sexuality to get our attention.

Sex Is Mysterious

Another reason sex has such influence is that it's mysterious. I've been married for a long time to Cathy; we have three grown girls, and there are still aspects of sexuality that are a mystery! I'm not sure there is a more profound mystery in the world. Every healthy person is curious about sex, and that's okay. When I speak at conferences and give the "sex talks," I'm always amazed at what a quiet and attentive audience I have. Is it because of my ability to communicate? I wish it were! It's because everyone is curious. Somehow we know there is beauty in the mystery of our sexuality. I think God made sex mysterious because He wanted us to keep it special. When sex quits being a mystery to you, it's time to worry.

Sex Is Fun

Now, this reason for sex being an influence in our lives might sound strange, but hear me out. Sex is fun. I can tell you from experience that sex is fun. God created sex to be enjoyable. I believe it gives Him great pleasure to provide His children with enjoyable experiences—and let's face it, sex is one of the all-time great experiences! I realize this is a bit blunt, but before you put the book down, let me explain. . . .

One reason people talk about sex so much is that it can be a wonderful experience. Don't be fooled, however, into thinking that all sex is fun. God wants the best for you, and that is why He asks you to save yourself for your marriage partner. And because premarital sex is not what God intended for us, it often becomes anything but fun. I've met guys and girls who have had some negative sexual experiences and will bear the scars for their entire lives. I'll talk more about sex outside of marriage later on in the book. The main point I want to get across right now is simply that we must be aware that sex is a major influence on our thinking, and a huge cause is the pleasure that it can bring us.

No one will disagree that sex has an influence on our lives, but now it is important for us to take a serious look at another important question: How does God view sex? Most of you reading this book believe in God, most of you want to please Him, and most of you honestly want to live according to His will. To find out how God views sex and what His will is, we need to find out what the Bible says.

What Does the Bible Say About Sex and Sexuality?

Many Christians need to erase certain ideas of what they think the Bible says about sex because, unfortunately, many of us were simply taught wrong! Well-meaning teachers communicated either directly or indirectly that sex is dirty, rotten, and ugly and that we should save this dirty, rotten, and ugly experience for marriage. Please get this straight right now: God doesn't view sex (or your desire for it) as dirty, rotten, or ugly!

God created your sexuality. Look at Genesis 2:18–25. It's the story of God creating Eve as a partner for Adam. Adam is ecstatic because the only companions he had before Eve were "all the beasts of the field and all the birds of the air" (v. 19). They may be great for pets, but they're not exactly what Adam had in mind for a lifelong partner. When Adam woke up from his little nap and met Eve for the first time, he was excited. As the Bible describes their relationship, it offers us a lesson: "Therefore a man leaves his father and his mother and cleaves to his wife, *and they become one flesh. And the man and his wife were both naked, and were not ashamed.*" (Genesis 2:24–25 RSV, emphasis added).

God created man and woman. He created their bodies, minds, and spirits. His hand was involved in *every* aspect of their being, and their sexuality was a big part of their being. Notice that when God created light, darkness, the earth, vegetation, stars, birds, fish, and animals, "God saw that it was good" (Genesis 1:25). After God created Adam and a partner for him, Eve, "God saw all that he had made, and it was *very* good" (Genesis 1:31, emphasis added).

In my opinion, any view other than the belief that God created sexuality and He sees it as *very* good is a warped view. The problem with our society's attitude toward sex is that it is incomplete. Because our sexuality was created by God, we should view it as His special gift to us.

Let's look at another passage from the Bible, this time from the New Testament:

> *Flee from sexual immorality. All other sins a man commits are outside his body, but he who sins sexually sins against his own body. Do you not know that your body is a temple of the Holy Spirit, who is in you, whom you have received from God? You are not your own; you were bought at a price. Therefore honor God with your body.*
> (1 Corinthians 6:18–20)

When I read this section of God's Word, a couple of points really jump off the page. First, our bodies are temples of God. The Holy Spirit of God actually dwells within our bodies. I take this to mean that our bodies are special and that we should treat them with respect and honor. This is true as we deal with our sexuality, decide how much we eat, or work on keeping our "temples" in shape physically.

The other point that jumps out of this passage is that we are to glorify God with our bodies. What you do with your body is one of the few things in life that is almost totally under your own control. You must choose whether to honor God or to dishonor Him with your body. A decision you make about sexual relations may or may not honor your Lord.

Let's face it, throughout our entire lives—even during old age—sex will influence us. The big question for you and me is *how* it will influence us. Make sure that you question the media's influence. Make sure you learn what God's desire for your sexuality is all about. Then you'll never have to settle for a counterfeit love, and you'll never accept anything less than the real thing.

Things to Think About

1. The media is mentioned as a major influence on our thinking about sex. Do you agree or disagree? Why?
2. What are specific ways to keep the strong sexual influence of the media out of our lives?
3. If God created sex and sees it as very good, why would He ask us to wait until marriage to enjoy it?
4. Why do you think the world is so interested in sex?

Respect Builders

1. The influence of sex in the media: For the next few days be especially alert to the ads you see on television and in newspapers and magazines.

- How many ads use sexuality in some way to promote their products?
- How many ads use women's bodies in some way?
- How many ads use men's bodies in some way?
- How many ads use both men's and women's bodies?
- How many ads suggest a sexual relationship between a man and a woman?

Sexuality is also found in the world of entertainment:

- Think about the last movie you saw—chances are that sex entered into the action, if not the plot! What message about relationships or sexuality did that movie communicate?

- Was that message healthy or unhealthy? Was it pleasing to God or not?

- Consider the television programs that are popular. Choose one series and jot down two or three points it teaches about sexuality.

An awareness of the nature of these teachers—the advertising, movie, and television industries—can help us not to be influenced by their messages, which often go against the teachings of the Bible.

2. During the next week, keep track of the various attitudes toward sex you hear and see acted out in the world around you. Write down the source and a brief description of each attitude. A couple of examples will start you off.

The Source	The Attitude
TV commercial	Sex sells a product.
Guys in the locker room	Sex is a conquest to brag about.

Team Effort

God created sex!

Here's an excellent group discussion starter:

1. Does the statement "God created sex" challenge any of your ideas about sex?
2. Have you somewhere picked up the idea that sex is dirty?
3. Ask God to help you see sex as His gift to you—a gift He wants you to save for marriage.
4. Read the following Scripture references. In your own words, summarize what they tell you about a biblical attitude toward sex.

Scripture	Summary in My Own Words
Genesis 2:20–25	
Proverbs 5:18–19	
Proverbs 18:22	
Song of Songs 5:10–16	
Song of Songs 7:1–9	
1 Corinthians 6:18–20	
1 Corinthians 7:3	
Hebrews 13:4	

Chapter Six

Sexual Intercourse

People have described sexual intercourse as thrilling, soul-stirring, boring, shocking, deeply satisfying, painful, wonderfully comfortable, disappointing, fascinating, disgusting, delightful—and the list could go on and on. In many surveys about sexuality, one of the top questions students have is wanting information about sexual intercourse.

Surveys also tell us that a majority of sixteen- to eighteen-year-olds have had sexual intercourse. This means that not only are people wanting information about sexual intercourse *before* they experience it, but that they are also interested *after* they've experienced it. We can also conclude that people may have sexual intercourse without understanding it.

I think it is healthy to want to learn about and to wonder about sex. Wondering what it would be like with your husband or wife is definitely not wrong or gross. In fact, it is very normal.

Wondering about sexual intercourse can lead us to want to know what God says about it. We may find that the Bible isn't filled with as many "do's and don'ts" as we sometimes think. The Bible clearly states, however, that sexual intercourse outside of marriage is not right in God's eyes. You've probably heard the words "adultery" and "fornication." Here is how *Webster's Collegiate Dictionary, Tenth Edition* defines these words. Adultery is "voluntary sexual intercourse between a married man and someone other than his wife or between a married woman and someone other than her husband." Fornication is "consensual sexual intercourse between two persons not married to each other."

As a high-school student who had recently become a Christian, I had many questions about sexuality, and I was frustrated because at times the Bible didn't seem clear enough. At other times, I questioned why the Bible seemed so old-fashioned in not allowing sex before marriage. Is God just the ultimate grinch when it comes to sexuality? Many people reading this book have similar questions. I want to help answer some of these questions by stating four reasons for sexual intercourse in marriage. These four reasons are not necessarily in any order; each one is, however, an important dimension of the role sex has in marriage.

The Role of Intercourse in Marriage

Unity: One Flesh

In a mysterious, almost sacred, sense, when two people have sexual intercourse they become one flesh. Even the physical act of sexual intercourse is symbolic of the oneness and unity of the couple. The Bible puts it this way: "For this reason a man will leave his father and mother and be united to his wife, *and they will become one flesh*" (Genesis 2:24 RSV, emphasis added; Jesus also quoted this passage in Matthew 19:4–6). This verse speaks of a real oneness in which a couple is so intimate that each person completely shares the other's nakedness. Interestingly, the next verse in Genesis says, "The man and his wife were both naked, and they felt no shame" (Genesis 2:25 RSV). This idea of unity as one flesh is seldom talked about today, yet it is a very special aspect of sexual intercourse.

Communication

Perhaps the deepest form of communication and love is sexual intercourse. It is during sexual intercourse that you and your partner are physically expressing and sharing your deepest love for one another. A certain tender feeling during this intimate experience communicates a sense of unconditional love, similar to the sacrificial love God has for humankind. During sex, you are communicating the deepest sense of commitment. Sex only for selfish pleasure is second-rate at best; it subtly communicates a strong message of disregard for the other person that can be quite hurtful.

Enjoyment

As I said in a previous chapter, sex is fun! In my opinion, there is nothing more enjoyable in the entire world than the shared experience of marital sex. In a recent counseling session, a sixteen-year-old girl was talking to me about her struggles with sex. Referring to her first time having sex, she said, "I didn't enjoy it at all. It was rushed, I was afraid, and the car was uncomfortable." That is *not* how sexual intercourse was meant to be. Sex was meant to be experienced in the relaxed, romantic, leisurely atmosphere of the marriage bed—not in the back seat of a car!

I feel sorry for the Puritans of our country in the late 1600s. Many of them actually believed that the only reason for sexual intercourse was "making babies." They were correct that intercourse can create another life, but it can be so much more than an act of procreation. The pure enjoyment, the intimate communication, and the symbolic and physical oneness of sex in a marriage make it one of the most special gifts God has ever given humankind.

Procreation

As I just mentioned, sex is also God's method of creating a child. It is a miracle designed by God. And I consider it one of His all-time greatest miracles and an all-around wonderful idea! The miracle of a man's sperm making contact with the woman's egg at precisely the right time to create life is an incredible occurrence! The beauty of two married people who love each other very much being an intricate part along with God in creating another life, blood of their blood, flesh of their flesh, is beyond the written or spoken word.

God's special purpose in creating sex was that two married people would produce an offspring from their own lives. It is a tragedy that more than a million *unwanted* pregnancies happen each year. It is a shame that something as wonderful as creating new life is taken lightly by many people in our generation. When two people believe they are mature enough to have sexual intercourse, as husband and wife, they should think through the eventual possibility of raising a child. If they haven't dealt with the issue of parenting, they haven't experienced intercourse as God intended humankind to experience it. I'm not saying that a husband and wife who aren't ready for kids shouldn't have sex until they are—but the chance of getting pregnant exists even when birth control is used, and couples should discuss this before walking down the aisle. The result of doing so is an added sense of comfort and freedom in their married sex life, because they are not afraid of a pregnancy tearing them apart. Having explored the Scriptures regarding premarital sex and intercourse with someone other than your spouse, I no longer view God as the "grinch who ruined sex." I understand that when you create something as special and meaningful as the intimacy of sexual intercourse, you clearly desire the very best for your creation. God knew that the best sex is shared by a man and a woman who love each other unconditionally and who are committed to making their relationship last a lifetime through marriage. I'm not saying that all sexual intercourse outside of marriage produces only negative feelings. I'd be lying to you if I said that. Instead, I'm saying, why settle for anything less than God's best, when it brings the true fulfillment sexual intercourse was designed to produce?

Things to Think About

1. Do the teenagers you know wish they had more information about sex?

2. About what other subjects in the area of sexuality do you think teenagers want more information?

3. Do you think I was right to include "enjoyment" as one of the reasons for sexual intercourse? Why or why not?

4. Do you agree or disagree with this statement on procreation: "When two people believe they are mature enough to have sexual intercourse, as husband and wife, they should think through the eventual possibility of raising a child. If they haven't dealt with the issue of parenting, they haven't experienced intercourse as God intended humankind to experience it"? Give reasons for your answer.

Respect Builder

1. This may sound like a difficult assignment! Ask a married adult whom you respect and trust to look at this chapter and give his or her opinions on the content. (This could be an excellent youth group assignment or good conversation with your parents.)

2. Think for a few moments about the ideas you have regarding sexual intercourse, where you got these ideas, and the reliability of your sources. Make a few notes on the following chart to help you get a clearer picture of how your attitudes have been affected by various influences around you. A couple of examples have been provided to get you started.

An Idea About Sexual Intercourse	Where I Got This Idea	Reliability of This Source
Sex is dirty. It's dumb to abstain.	Graffiti Friends	Poor They don't really know any more than I do.

Team Effort

A Bible study on becoming one flesh:
Jesus quoted the Old Testament when He said:

> *Haven't you read . . . that at the beginning the Creator "made them male and female," and said, "For this reason a man will leave his father and mother and be united to his wife, and the two will become one flesh"? So they are no longer two, but one. Therefore what God has joined together, let man not separate.* (Matthew 19:4–6)

Discuss these questions:

1. How does this Scripture describe the mysterious unity between a man and a woman?
2. How is the actual physical act of intercourse a graphic illustration of being one flesh?
3. How does this Scripture go against the world's popular philosophy of casual sex?
4. Why do you think God created sexual intercourse as the method of creating a child?
5. What other insights can you receive from this powerful passage of Scripture?

For a deeper biblical look at the subject of sexual immorality, you may want to check out the verses that follow. You're probably familiar with some of them. (Note: Some versions of the Bible use the word "fornication" to translate the Greek word that is common to all these Scriptures. Remember, that word means any sexual intercourse between people who are not married to each other.) What do these verses say about sexual immorality?

1 Corinthians 5:9–11

1 Corinthians 6:12–20

1 Corinthians 7:1–3

Galatians 5:19–21

Ephesians 5:3

Colossians 3:5

1 Thessalonians 4:3

Do you get the feeling that people in the ancient world had as much trouble handling their hormones as people do today?

Chapter Seven

Differences in the Way
Men and Women Respond

"Guys can be such perverts! All my boyfriend ever thinks about is sex. I'm not a Goody-Two-Shoes, but I really want to know: Are there guys in this world who think about anything other than sex?"

I get a question like this at every seminar I teach on sex. And the answer to this girl's question is yes *and* no. Of course guys think about things other than sex. But most healthy adolescent boys can easily spend a lot of time thinking about sex.

It seems to me that besides the obvious physical differences between male and female human beings, some other significant differences are important to discuss—and the question in the previous paragraph points to one such difference. You can attribute these differences to biology, cultural conditioning, or whatever you like, but acknowledging some of these basic differences might help you understand why your boyfriend or girlfriend acts the way he or she does.

Many experts in the field of sex and dating say that one critical difference between the male and female has to do with the relationship of sex and love. I've heard Josh McDowell, a popular Christian speaker, say in presentations, "I'm convinced sex is more dominant in the mind of a man and love is more paramount in the mind of a woman." When a couple goes to a romantic movie, often the male thinks "sex" and the female thinks "love." After the first romantic scene, the male is ready to park at Inspiration Point and miss the rest of the movie. The female responds more to the idea of love and the beauty of romance. The female is much more interested in the love story while the male is more interested in a replay of the action—now!

As you can see, like Josh McDowell, I'm also convinced that the subject of sex is more often dominant in the minds of guys and love is more dominant in the minds of girls. It's not that girls aren't interested in sex or guys in love, but there is a difference. Perhaps the difference stems from what stimulates (or turns on) a guy and a girl. A guy is usually ready for sex any time, any place, at a moment's notice. A girl, on the other hand, is stimulated by romantic movies, flowers, or a slight touch on the shoulder. Guys are stimulated by sight, girls by touch. Of course, I'm speaking in generalities!

Guys can be sexually aroused in a matter of seconds. (I'm serious!) It takes girls longer. I've often compared a male's sex drive to a drum solo by your favorite rock band. The male sex drive is intense. It builds quickly to a climax, explodes with excitement, and then ends as quickly as it started. A woman's sex drive is more like a Bach concerto. It takes a little longer to get going. It builds to a tremendous climax, slowly settles down, and then ends softly. Why do I mention these differences? To help you understand and perhaps think more carefully about your actions when it comes to sexual stimulation.

If, for instance, you girls could only understand what you are doing to us guys with what you wear or don't wear! Remember, a guy is stimulated by sight. Now, I'm not recommending turtleneck sweaters and ankle-length gowns for the beach. I am advising, however, that when you get dressed for a date, remember that what you are wearing can definitely help create a mood and atmosphere for your time together.

I'm convinced that most of the time girls just do not think about or even realize what they are doing to guys when they dress in certain ways. I'll never forget a time when sixteen kids from my youth group took a week-long houseboat trip. The first night, several of the girls came into the kitchen to visit us guys as we were playing a game at the table. The girls were wearing long T-shirts—and that was practically it. No bras, and nothing over their panties. After the girls moved on through the kitchen, the guys went absolutely crazy. Their minds had definitely shifted from concentrating on the game to thoughts about something else!

I decided not to make a big deal of it but to talk to the girls about what turns guys on. At the right time, we had a wonderful talk. I'm convinced those girls simply had not thought that what they were wearing would turn those guys on. When it comes to how a girl dresses or acts around guys, she must continually think through how guys react, especially if she wants to steer clear of trouble.

Guys also need to be careful about what they wear and what they say and do. Girls are attracted by sight, but they are also attracted by touch and talk. Guys need to be careful about what they say to girls. I have a friend who told his girlfriend on the second date that he loved her. The problem was that she believed him! She fell madly and passionately in love with him. When he saw what those powerful three words did to her, he backed down and tried to explain: "I didn't mean 'love'!" Ladies, you can probably imagine how devastated that poor girl was.

What I'm trying to say is that males and females respond differently when it comes to sexuality. Of course, there are also many similarities in their responses, but one of the smartest things you can do is to be aware of the basic differences. Think through your actions and avoid any position that might cause frustration to others. Once you're sensitive to these differences between men and women, you needn't be threatened by them. You may even be able to see how these differences enrich your relationships with members of the opposite sex.

Things to Think About

1. Do you agree that, in general, guys are more motivated by sex and girls more motivated by love?
2. What things do you think girls do or wear that stimulate guys?
3. What things do you think guys do or wear that stimulate girls?
4. Do you think it is important to understand some of the differences between males and females? Why or why not?

Respect Builders

1. After reading this chapter, list the observations I shared, and then list your own thoughts about the differences between men and women.

	How Men Respond	How Women Respond
Jim's Observations		
My Observations and Thoughts		

Now list several aspects of the opposite sex that could possibly give you romantic or sexual feelings toward them.

2. Based on the differences between men and women discussed in this chapter, what are some things you might need to do differently in your relationships with members of the opposite sex? Make a list and begin working on it this week.

Team Effort

The following two ideas are great ways to gain a better awareness of the differences between men and women. These ideas can be used separately or they can be used together.

1. Separate into two groups—guys and girls. In your group, brain-storm about the characteristics your ideal boyfriend or girlfriend would possess. Then come together and share your ideas. Discuss any differences or similarities between the two groups.
2. Assemble a panel comprised of the following people: a single male, a single female, and a married couple. Have the students ask the panel any questions they have about dating or marriage. To help get the discussion started, prepare some questions in advance.

Chapter Eight

How to Know if You Are in Love

Recently, I watched a group of high-school girls on the beach check out a handsome lifeguard. (Who says guys are the only ones who look at the scenery on the beach?) As the lifeguard leisurely walked to the water to cool off, the girls went crazy with excitement! One of the girls making the most noise sighed and exclaimed, "That guy's a total hottie! I think I'm in love!"

I don't think her reaction was unusual—in fact, it was quite normal. I even remember saying very similar words when I was in high school and college. (Not about male lifeguards, of course!) Let's think about the girl's remarks, though. The lifeguard may have been a "hottie," but I doubt the girl was really "in love." She was "in infatuation." She was attracted to this young lifeguard on a physical level. Perhaps she even had a fantasy of walking hand in hand with him down the beach at sunset. But was she "in love"? Not at all.

I remember my first crush. Her name was Geri. She was absolutely beautiful. I was totally convinced that someday we would walk down the aisle together. I think I liked her most because she was a better baseball player than I was, and she was also the only girl in elementary school who would play sports with us guys! I liked her for years. In fact, once in junior high, I wrote a note to her and signed it: "I love you." From that day on, she hardly ever talked to me! I think I scared her away. Was that love? No, it was infatuation. It was what is sometimes called "puppy love." But, hey, puppy love is real to puppies!

Infatuation and crushes are a normal part of life. Infatuation involves many of the same emotions and feelings real love does. The major difference between love and infatuation is that real love stands the test of time.

From the moment I met Cathy, I was attracted to her. In fact, I was infatuated with her. I knew that I loved her, though, when I was still attracted to her after two and a half years of dating. Furthermore, I was *committed* to her. When I first met her, I never imagined she had the normal human faults everyone else has. I imagined that she and our relationship were perfect. As time went on, I saw otherwise. Neither of us was (or is) perfect. The relationship wasn't perfect, and it wasn't always easy. When even after an argument I still cared deeply for Cathy, I knew that this was becoming more than infatuation. Real love stands the test of disagreements and of time.

There is no easy way to determine whether you are in love for keeps or not. If you are a teenager, something to think about is a statistic I've already mentioned: It is quite possible that you will "fall in love" about five times between ninth grade and your second year of college. As a teenager, you will experience various degrees of love, but the odds are against you marrying your high-school sweetheart and living happily ever after. I'm not saying it doesn't happen; I am just saying that the statistical odds are against it.

As I said before, there are no simple answers to the important question, "How do I know I'm in love?" I do, however, want to give you a few practical guidelines to help you decide if a certain person might be "the one"!

1. Do you have a selfless love or a selfish love?

True love is selfless love. Even when you are tired or have had a bad day, selfless love will enable you to meet the needs of your partner. A selfless love wants the very best for the other person even if it means waiting in the physical part of the relationship. A selfish love grows old quickly when its own needs are not being met. Far too many relationships in high school and even college are more selfish than selfless. If the person is always asking, "What's in it for me?" it is not a selfless love.

2. Do you like the other person?

I'll never forget a scene in the old-time classic movie *Shenandoah*. One young man approached the father of the woman he wanted to marry to ask for his daughter's hand in marriage. The father asked, "Do you like my daughter?" The young man answered, "I love your daughter." The wise old father said, "I didn't ask you if you loved her. I asked you, 'Do you like her?' "

Sometimes people get married even though they don't like the personality or behavior of their spouse. Often they think they'll change the other person. This plan is rarely successful. So ask yourself if you like your partner even with his or her faults. And consider whether you could live with his or her faults *forever*!

3. Are you transparent with each other?

Is your relationship one in which you can be open and honest with each other? Open communication is one of the major tools in a positive relationship. I've never seen a good relationship that didn't have this element of transparency.

4. Are you and your girlfriend/boyfriend too dependent on each other?

There are two kinds of relationships: "I love, therefore I need" and "I need, therefore I love." The second kind can be a real loser in the long run. Sadly, many relationships are based on this "I need, therefore I love" idea, and these usually end up going down the drain. Either one person ceases to "need" and therefore ceases to "love," or the other person gets tired of this total dependency and eventually leaves.

5. Is your relationship more about getting or giving?

When a person is infatuated with someone, that person is often asking, "What's in it for me?" This kind of love involves *getting* rather than *giving*. A self-centered love is not a true love; it is a counterfeit love. Our goal in love should be what the Greeks termed *agape* love: a love that has no strings attached. It's the same kind of self-giving, self-sacrificing love God has for you.

6. Are you and your special friend committed to the Purity Code?

A mutual commitment to the Purity Code will keep you together with a healthy relationship and ensure that you are making the kind of decisions God would want you to make. If only one of the people is committed to the Code, the relationship is most likely more about infatuation than love.

7. Do you have a mature love for Jesus Christ?

I believe that a good test of true love is to ask if both people involved can honestly say, "I have a desire to be all that God wants me to be. I am willing to put the Lord Jesus Christ first in my own life and in my friend's life. Our relationship to each other is second to my relationship with Christ." The couples I know who are doing well are those who have a good relationship with God individually and together as a couple. A love that is tied together with the love of God is the strongest kind of love.

I would suggest that you take a good hard look at the kind of love Paul talks about in 1 Corinthians 13. The qualities of love he describes in his "love chapter" can be a measuring stick to help you examine if you really are in love. When reading chapter 13, look especially at the qualities of love in verses 4–7.

> *Love is patient, love is kind. It does not envy, it does not boast, it is not proud. It is not rude, it is not self-seeking, it is not easily angered, it keeps no record of wrongs. Love does not delight in evil but rejoices with the truth. It always protects, always trusts, always hopes, always perseveres.*

This definition of love Paul offers here can help you honestly evaluate your love for another person.

Love is a uniquely wonderful experience. Unfortunately, the genuine experience of love can be closely imitated by an experience of infatuation. As time passes and presents us with storms to weather and new perspectives on our lives, we can then better distinguish between infatuation and real love. Right now, I think it could be important for you to deal with the questions I present here, study the ideals of love Paul sets forth, and trust God to show you His desire for your relationship. And, as trite as it sounds, time is on your side.

Things to Think About

1. What are some differences between love and infatuation?
2. Do you think most students are experiencing love or infatuation?
3. Is infatuation wrong? Why or why not?
4. Read 1 Corinthians 13:4–7. What impresses you about these qualities of love?

Respect Builders

1. Have you ever thought about the qualities you like and dislike in people of the opposite sex? Try it now!

Qualities I Like	Qualities I Dislike

Go back and put an X by the qualities you dislike so much that you're pretty sure you couldn't live happily with a person who had those qualities. Put an asterisk (*) by the positive qualities you think are most important in a person with whom you would want to share the rest of your life. Now you have a more objective way of evaluating relationships.

If you're dating a person who has none of the qualities you really like and several of the qualities you most dislike, you might want to ask yourself why you're dating him or her. And if you're dating someone who has many of the qualities you like and only a few of the qualities you mildly dislike, congratulations! You've made a good choice!

2. Consider the two kinds of relationships I mentioned in this chapter:

I love, therefore I need,
and
I need, therefore I love.

Under the headings following, write a sentence expressing your understanding of each kind of relationship. Also jot down some pros and cons for each kind of relationship. Then write in the initials of some people you know whose relationships fit the categories.

	"I love, therefore I need."	"I need, therefore I love."
Definition		
Pros		
Cons		
Initials		

Team Effort

God's Word gives a beautiful description of love in 1 Corinthians 13:4–7. Open your Bible to this passage. In the space that follows, write one phrase on each line. Then write in the actions of Jesus, of other biblical characters, or of people you know who illustrate these qualities of love. Discuss these qualities as a group. The first two have been done as an example.

Description	Illustration
Love is patient.	Jesus taught the disciples even when they were slow to believe His resurrection (see Luke 24:13–27).
Love is kind.	My friend helped me figure out my homework assignment even though she had a lot of her own work to do.

Description	Illustration

Close by praying that God will teach you to love your girlfriend or boyfriend, your family, and your other friends with the kind of love Paul describes.

Chapter Nine

Unconditional Love

Once upon a time, there was a young girl named Ashley. She was a beautiful little girl and had the most wonderful doll collection in the world. Her father traveled all over the world on business, and for nearly twelve years he had brought dolls home to Ashley. In her bedroom, she had shelves of dolls from throughout the United States and from every continent. She had dolls that could sing and dance and do just about anything a doll could possibly do.

One day, one of her father's business acquaintances came to visit. During dinner he asked Ashley about her wonderful doll collection. After they ate, Ashley took him by the hand and showed him these marvelous dolls from all over the world. He was very impressed. After he took the "grand tour" and was introduced to many of the beautiful dolls, he asked Ashley, "With all these precious dolls, you must have one that is your favorite. Which one is it?"

Without a moment's hesitation, Ashley went over to her old beat-up toy box and started pulling out toys. From the bottom of the box, she pulled out one of the most ragged dolls you have ever seen. Only a few strands of hair were left on its head. The clothing had long since disappeared. The doll was filthy from many years of playing outside with it. One of the buttons for the eyes was hanging down, connected by only a string. Stuffing was coming out at the elbows and knees. Ashley handed the doll to the gentleman and said, "This is my favorite."

The man was shocked and asked, "Why this doll, with all these beautiful dolls in your room?"

Ashley replied, "If I didn't love this doll, nobody would!"

That simple statement moved the businessman to tears. It was simple yet very profound. The little girl loved her doll unconditionally. She loved the doll not for its beauty or abilities, but simply because it was her very own doll.

In this same way, God loves you unconditionally, not for what you do but for who you are. You are His child. Millions of people in the world miss the simple fact that they are loved unconditionally by God. God accepts you. He believes in you and He wants the best for you.

Sometimes we feel that we don't deserve God's love. Sometimes we can't understand how God could have such patience with us when we continually mess up. Well, listen to this: *God's ways are different from our ways.* He doesn't love you only if you do certain things or live a certain lifestyle. He loves you—period! When people finally understand the depth of God's love, they are free to be all that He wants them to be. Interestingly, people who comprehend this unconditional love have an easier time staying away from the sin that can clog their relationships with God.

A perfect illustration of God's unconditional love is found in the story of the prodigal son, which Jesus told in Luke 15:11–32.

The parable opens with a man's younger son asking for his share of his father's property. Receiving half of the estate, the young man then goes to a distant country and proceeds to squander the wealth. Soon finding himself without a penny to his name in a country struck by a famine, the boy returns to his father's home. His father sees him from a distance and runs to greet him with open arms. The son's first words are, "Father, I have sinned against heaven and against you. I am no longer worthy to be called your son" (v. 21). The father's joyful reaction to his son's return, however, is to feast and celebrate because, in this loving father's words, "For this son of mine was dead and is alive again; he was lost and is found" (v. 24).

The son definitely sinned against his father. He wasted his money living wildly and immorally. Yet look at what happened when the son asked to come home as a hired hand! The father realized how the son had sinned, but he took his son back with open arms. The father joyfully celebrated the return of his wayward boy.

The reason this story is so fitting in a book on sex is that many of us have had a little trouble handling our hormones. We've struggled with the biblical standard of sexuality. At times, we've even turned our backs on God and gone our own way. But the good news is that no matter what we've done or how we've strayed, God waits for us with open arms. He loves all His children, and nothing in the world makes Him happier than for one of His children to wise up and come back to Him. Be assured that when we do go to Him, He receives us with a depth of love beyond human comprehension.

Before leaving this topic, let's review a few facts about the unconditional love of God.

God's Unconditional Love

God Loves You Not for What You Do, But for Who You Are

Sometimes this concept is difficult to understand, but it is true that you are deeply loved by God. He created you and He loves His creation. Even if you have turned your back on Him, He is there, like the father in the story of the prodigal son, with open arms and warm acceptance. Remember that the Christian faith is not based on rules and regulations; the Christian faith is based on a relationship between God and you. And remember that God never changes this desire to have a relationship with you, no matter what you do. When a person understands that God's love is not contingent on his or her actions, that person's life can be radically different.

God's Ways Are Different From Our Ways

One of the reasons we have so much trouble accepting God's love is that it is often contrary to what we know on a human level. In life, we must often *earn* acceptance by trying out for the baseball team or getting good grades or measuring up to some standards, either real or imagined. But God's love is there no matter what we do or don't do. God loves the drunk sleeping in the gutter in New York City as much as He loves you, and He loves the well-known ministry leader no more than He loves you. God cherishes each one of His creations.

God Loves You Sacrificially

God's deep and piercing love for you cost Him the life of His only Son. The ultimate sacrifice of Jesus dying on the cross so that you might have abundant life on earth and eternal life afterward is the greatest demonstration of love the world has ever known. The apostle Paul put it this way: "But God demonstrates his own love for us in this: While we were still sinners, Christ died for us" (Romans 5:8).

The Gift of God's Love Is Free

All you have to do is accept God's gift of love. One of the hardest things in life is to accept love we feel we don't deserve, but when we do, we can't help but be transformed by God's unconditional and overflowing love for us. As we begin to realize that we are loved despite our mistakes, this deep love will draw us even closer to God.

Things to Think About

1. How did you react to the story of Ashley and her doll collection?
2. Why do you think people have such a difficult time accepting God's unconditional love?
3. Can you relate to the story of the prodigal son mentioned in this chapter? If so, how?
4. Do you think it was important to include a chapter on unconditional love in this book? Why or why not?

Respect Builders

1. God loves you not for what you do but for who you are. Isn't that an amazing statement? Many of us are conditioned to receive love only if we're "good": "Mom won't love you if you keep hitting your sister" or "God won't love you if you sin." When you have

that system of thinking, you can change your behavior to receive love. But God turns this around: He loves you, and as you receive that love He enables you to change your behavior.

Check the following Scripture references and fill in the appropriate columns of the chart. It's okay if you have to leave some of the columns blank for some of the verses.

	Because God	He . . .	We respond by . . .
John 3:16	loved the world	gave His Son	believing in Him
John 3:17–18			
1 John 3:16			
1 John 4:7–12			
1 John 4:19–21			

2. The gift of God's unconditional love is free. Note the word "gift" in the following verse: "The gift of God is eternal life in Christ Jesus our Lord" (Romans 6:23). We don't earn it, deserve it, or buy it. All we can do is receive it.

If you have not yet entered into a relationship with God by accepting His gift of love, please give it serious consideration right now. It's the most important decision you will ever make. And the step is a simple one. You need only to acknowledge Him with words like these:

"Dear God, thank you for loving me. Thank you for loving me so much that you sent your Son to die for me and to save me from eternal punishment for my sins. Thank you for offering me the gift of eternal life instead."

If you have accepted that gift of eternal life—rejoice! And think of a way to thank God for it and share it with someone who does not have it.

Team Effort

God's ways are different from our ways. Isaiah affirms this statement. Look up Isaiah 55:8–9 and rewrite the verses in your own words. Or if you're more of a picture person than a word person, draw a sketch or cartoon to illustrate the verses.

Now think of some specific instances that show how God's ways are different from human ways. List some differences in the following chart. I've started the list for you. Share this with your family or group.

God's Ways	Human Ways
God wants us to save sexual intercourse for marriage.	Today, people don't wait. Many people also have sex outside of their marriages.
God calls us to love our enemies.	
Jesus gives us the commandment to love our neighbor as ourselves.	
We are to live as servants.	

In talking about God's unconditional love, I referred to the story Jesus told about the son who left home. Let's take another look at that story. Review that part of the chapter or read Luke 15:11–24, and then follow the instructions below.

List everything the younger son and the father did.

Younger Son	Father

Use an exclamation point (!) to mark the actions of the father that show his unconditional love for his son.

Jesus told this story and two others to show God's response to sinners who repent. Read the other two stories in Luke 15:1–10. Taken together, what do these three stories tell you about God the Father and His response to sinful human beings?

Chapter Ten

Peer Pressure

No one is exempt from peer pressure. This demand to conform to a particular group or to society in general is made on people of all ages. The pressure to conform comes in various shapes and sizes. Sometimes it is subtle; sometimes it is blatant. No one having a heartbeat, though, can say that he or she has never had to wrestle with peer pressure.

Peer pressure can often be a spiritual dilemma involving the struggle between the spirit and the flesh (the sinful nature in all of us). If you for one moment think you are the only one fighting this battle, you are wrong. Even the apostle Paul suffered deeply from this war within. Listen to him talk about his struggle:

> *I do not understand what I do. For what I want to do I do not do, but what I hate I do…. I know that nothing good lives in me, that is, in my sinful nature. For I have the desire to do what is good, but I cannot carry it out. For what I do is not the good I want to do; no,*

*the evil I do not want to do—this I keep on doing. Now if I do what
I do not want to do, it is no longer I who do it, but it is sin living in
me that does it.* (Romans 7:15, 18–20)

I think Paul was a lot like you and me. He made mistakes and he
often missed the mark, but by no means was he an evil person. His
deepest desire was to do right. He didn't want to settle for second best,
but at times he blew it. His insight about his failings was brilliant.
He was able to see this problem for what it actually was—*a spiritual
battle.* He really did want to do right, yet he kept messing up. At the
end of his little discourse, he answered his own question: "Who will
rescue me from this body of death? Thanks be to God—through
Jesus Christ our Lord!" (Romans 7:24–25). For Paul, the solution to
the problem of being pressured to conform to the world's standards
came from Jesus Christ. Paul didn't spiritualize the issue and tell his
readers that his problems were finished forever. He simply knew *who*
would help him in the fight.

It's an undeniable reality of life that temptations will come and
go, but like Paul, you can be confident that God will help you work
through the temptations when you seek His help. Paul wrote to a
group of people in the city of Corinth and said:

*No temptation has seized you except what is common to man.
And God is faithful; he will not let you be tempted beyond what you
can bear. But when you are tempted, he will also provide a way out
so that you can stand up under it.* (1 Corinthians 10:13)

In Christ, you have the power to deal with peer pressure. Here
are a few suggestions that can make the battle a little easier.

Suggestions to Ease the Battle

Don't Let Peer Pressure Sneak Up on You

Use your head! Know when you are being pressured to conform to a standard that is second best! Face the pressure and carefully think about the possible outcome of your action. Ask questions such as these: "Am I settling for second best?" "Will my actions be pleasing to God?" "Am I being pressured to do something that I feel isn't right?" Sometimes by thinking logically and looking at all the options, we can find it easier to overcome a temptation.

Remember That Everyone You Spend Time With Has an Influence on You

It always fascinates me when I watch groups or cliques of people hanging around with each other. If one person in the group likes a certain kind of music, usually the others will also like that kind of music. If one person wears a certain style of clothes, others in the group will probably wear that same style. Our friends play an important part in determining who we are, what we stand for, and where we are going in life. That's why it is important to choose our friends wisely.

God's Word has much to say about friends and companions. Proverbs 22:24–25, for instance, offers us this lesson: "Do not make friends with a hot-tempered man, do not associate with one easily angered, or you may learn his ways and get yourself ensnared." It's all too easy to pick up bad habits from friends. On the other hand, the right kind of friends can influence us toward bettering our lives: "As iron sharpens iron, so one man sharpens another" (Proverbs 27:17).

Perhaps you need to take an inventory of your friends. Ask yourself:

1. Are my friends a positive or a negative influence on my life?
2. Are my friends helping me to be all that God wants me to be, or are they tearing me down?
3. What kind of influence do my friends have on my life?

If your answers show that your friends are a negative influence, it is time to make some major decisions about your friendships. Remember, "He who walks with the wise grows wise, but a companion of fools suffers harm" (Proverbs 13:20).

Choose Your Friends Wisely

I had a friend named Alex. We used to talk for hours. He had a strong desire to do right. He wanted to be a professional baseball player, he wanted to get good grades, and he wanted girls to like him. Alex also had a strong desire to be a growing Christian. He would talk and fantasize about baseball and these other dreams, yet he never seemed to achieve any of his goals. He was always falling down and failing.

Finally, after months of struggling, Alex offered me an insight into his problems when he told me about his "flaky friends" and how they would always bring him down. I said, "You know, it's your choice to be so influenced by those friends. Why don't you spend a little less time with them and a little more time with Kevin and Tim?" Alex had told me earlier that Kevin and Tim were very good influences on him.

Alex took my advice. He still spent time with his old, undependable friends, but he began to *choose* to spend more and more time with Kevin and Tim. You can guess what happened. Every area of his life began to improve. Because of Tim and Kevin's influence, Alex was motivated to get his act together. He couldn't kick the negative influence of peer pressure on his own, but he chose to be influenced by positive peer pressure. And that made all the difference for him.

Remember Your Uniqueness: You Are Special in God's Eyes

Never forget that *God loves you for who you are, not for what you do.* You are a special person in God's eyes. Because of His unconditional love, you are free to be all that He created you to be! Jesus said, "You will know the truth, and the truth will set you free" (John 8:32). A person who truly understands that he or she is loved by God will not be as motivated to conform to peer pressure. He or she instead understands what it is to be accepted by the One whose acceptance is truly important: God himself.

Seek First the Kingdom of God

In the midst of our daily activities and responsibilities, it is easy to get distracted. Jesus gave us some sound advice when He said, "But seek first his kingdom and his righteousness, and all these things will be given to you as well" (Matthew 6:33). If we put God first, He will provide the necessities of life. Unfortunately, we often worry more about what people think than about what God wants for us.

An important factor in overcoming the pull of negative peer pressure is to possess the inner strength that comes from having a healthy self-image. When you put God first in your life, you can develop that stronger self-image. After all, you were created in *His* image! And although you are flawed by sin, He values you so much that He sent Christ to die for you. As you develop this improved self-image, you gain inner strength and then you are better able to say no to peer pressure.

Interestingly enough, the people I know who overcome peer pressure are people who are more concerned about seeking God than they are about pleasing their friends, classmates, or co-workers. They are seeking first His kingdom. In fact, as they do that, they seem to have better relationships with their friends than anyone else I know.

It's Hard to Say No

Another topic related to peer pressure and sex and dating is the "it's hard to say no" problem. Many young people have been pressured into experiencing sex when they really didn't want to—simply because they didn't know how to say no. I've talked to a number of people who have really regretted not saying "no thanks" before it was too late.

In his book on teenage sexuality, Aaron Haas reports the results of his survey of teenagers' sexual attitudes. His findings on the subject of saying no are enlightening. Teenagers were asked, for instance, "Have there been times when you have been on a date, when you had sexual contact even though you really did not feel like it?" Forty-three percent of the guys who were ages fifteen and sixteen and a whopping 65 percent of the girls of the same age answered yes. Nearly half of the guys and more than half of the girls who were ages fifteen and sixteen had had a difficult time saying "No thanks."[1]

What were the reasons these young people gave for acting contrary to their true feelings? Here are some of the answers and circumstances explained to Dr. Haas:

"I didn't want to hurt his/her feelings."

"I didn't want him/her to think I was a prude!"

"I really felt pressured."

"I just couldn't say 'No!' "

"I was afraid that he/she wouldn't like me if I said 'No!' "

"I don't know why, but I felt obligated to go along with
   him/her."

"I was high" or "I was drunk!"

"It meant a lot to him and not much to me."

"I didn't want to seem like a tease."

"I was afraid she would think I didn't like her."

"I wanted to prove I was a man."

"I did it for the experience."

"There was nothing else to do."

As many of these statements show, insecurity and self-esteem play a major role in how people respond to peer pressure. They can be afraid to say no. They don't want to hurt someone's feelings. And they don't want to be ridiculed for their decision. I think, however, that any boyfriend or girlfriend who is worth keeping will greatly respect your ability to say "no thanks." If the other person is only interested in your body, then he or she isn't worth keeping. It really is hard to say no, but it's always worth it.

Before concluding this chapter, I want to list a few of the lines and lies guys and girls use on each other. In print they look absurd, but in the heat of passion they seem to make sense. When sexual feelings are running high, even the most honest person may become desperate and try to manipulate another person. Although we could probably come up with a different line for every day of the year, I'll mention only a few of the key ideas that seem to be used over and over.

1. "It's okay if we both agree to do it."

Usually one person in a relationship is more eager to become sexually involved than the other. If he or she can get the other person to agree verbally, then that seems to make the action okay.

2. "You're the only person I will ever love, so let's not wait until we're married."

This argument is powerful, but in most cases it simply isn't true. The average person has at least five loves during the teenage years and early twenties. Because this statement about never loving anyone else again is usually false, it's a ridiculous line for someone to use— especially when it's said to convince a person to do something they don't want to do.

3. "If you really love me . . ."

This is the "you've got to prove your love to me" line: "If you really love me, prove it." This line is most successfully used by manipulative older guys who are dating younger girls. For people with low self-esteem, this line can be one of the hardest to handle. Too many people allow their emotional involvement with a person to exceed their maturity level. Don't fall for this one.

4. "Let's experiment to see what it's like. If we don't like it, we'll never have to do it again."

People actually fall for this! The aggressor knows that if the partner gives approval once, he or she will most likely give in again at other times. Remember that it's harder to say no the second time.

5. "Everybody's doing it. Are you a freak or something?"

First let me say, "Wrong! Everybody isn't doing it!" On any junior-high, high-school, or college campus, people have chosen not to be sexually active—and often they are the real leaders in the school. Thousands have chosen to live by the Purity Code. You are not a freak if you choose not to engage in sexual promiscuity. Don't give in to peer pressure because of a flimsy line like this one!

6. "If it happens, it happens!"

These words are usually said by the person who is always raising the subject of sex. Be careful of people who are always raising philosophical questions about sex, asking personal questions about your sex life, and harping on the subject so much that it would be easy to be tempted. This line is a sly one, but it works—just ask thousands of disappointed girls and guys who fell for it.

Peer pressure is real. It's a fact of life we all must deal with at any age, but the pressure seems much more difficult to handle at certain times of our lives. I know that peer pressure combined with a poor self-image and a deep love for another person can cause us to do things we might later regret. We can deal with this pressure more easily when we choose friends who will be supportive of us. It also helps to spend time considering God's love for us. Trust in this love and rely on God's promises to be with you as you face temptations and pressure from your peers.

Things to Think About

1. Why is it so difficult to fight the battle of peer pressure?
2. Why do you think so many people have such a problem saying no to sex even when they don't want to have it?
3. Do you agree or disagree with the idea that the people you spend time with have a profound influence on you? Why?
4. What makes you unique in God's eyes?

Respect Builders

1. Choose your friends wisely. Remember, this doesn't necessarily mean you will totally drop someone who is having a bad influence on you. That person may need the *good* influence for Christ that you can offer to him or her. But you might want to find a better balance of time spent with that person and time spent with people who are good influences.

   Write down the initials of people with whom you spend time. Then use a + or a - to indicate whether each person is, in general, a good or bad influence. Then determine roughly what percentage of your time is spent with each person, and write the figures in the third column.

The People	The Influence	The Time

Looking at the previous chart, what change in the percentages you've written do you think you might need to make?

2. Everyone you spend time with has an influence on you. Scripture has much to say about the way friends can influence us for good or for bad. Read the Scripture references indicated here and summarize what each one says about the good or bad influence of friends.

	A Friend's Good Influence	A Friend's Bad Influence
Proverbs 13:20		
Proverbs 17:17		
Proverbs 18:24		
Proverbs 22:24–25		
Proverbs 27:17		

Now think seriously about the people with whom you spend the most time.

How are my friends influencing me?	How am I influencing my friends?

Look at the way you completed the chart. Do you need to make some changes in the amount of time you spend with certain people or in the way you allow yourself to respond to those people? Be specific—don't answer with just a yes or no!

Team Effort

It's hard to say no.

Sometimes it helps if you think through an answer before you need it. The following statements are some of the most popular lines people of both sexes use to try to manipulate another person into sexual activity. Think through each statement and come up with a response. Your responses may be logical, witty, or outrageous—whatever you want them to be. Share your responses with the group.

1. "It's okay if we both agree to do it."
2. "You're the only person I will ever love, so let's not wait until we're married."
3. "If you really love me, you will do it."
4. "Let's experiment to see what it's like. If we don't like it, we'll never have to do it again."
5. "Everybody's doing it! What's wrong with you?"
6. "If it happens, it happens!"

Having thought about these arguments, you're probably now better prepared to deal with one if it ever comes your way!

Chapter Eleven

Radical Respect

Jason and Jennifer were boyfriend and girlfriend. They had been dating for seven months. One day when I was speaking at a Purity Code sexuality event for high-school students, I used them as an illustration. I didn't know them before the event, and little did I know that my illustration would affect their relationship forever. I wanted to get the point across that as Christians, we are called to "radically respect" our boyfriends or girlfriends. I wanted the crowd to understand that because we are Christians we are to treat each other as if Jesus lived in each believer. Why? Because He actually does. Check out 1 Corinthians 6:19:

> *Do you not know that your body is a temple of the Holy Spirit, who is in you, whom you have received from God? You are not your own.*

I looked around the room for a couple holding hands. I picked out Jason and Jennifer. I asked, "Have you two been dating?" They nodded yes. I asked their names. Then I said, "Jason, you are not just dating Jennifer, who is very beautiful, has a wonderful personality, and is a Christian, but you are dating the Jesus who lives inside Jennifer. Treat her with a radical respect. She is a child of God. And Jennifer [she blushed], you aren't just dating Jason, an outgoing guy, a real hunk, and a Christian, but according to the Bible, you are dating the Jesus who lives inside Jason. Jason is a very special child of God. You are to respect him as if Jesus were present in his life."

These two beautiful people just smiled and I went on with my point. However, six months later I got an e-mail from Jason to say thanks. He said that he and Jennifer had been about one week from going all the way, and they had never thought of treating each other with the radical respect I'd described. That very day, they decided to treat each other as God would want, and they did not have sexual intercourse.

The apostle Paul's advice to us is to "outdo one another in showing honor" (Romans 12:10 RSV). The Christian approach to dating and relating to the opposite sex must be radically different from what we see in the secular media. We are to treat each other as children of God. Jesus Christ lives with each believer by the power of the Holy Spirit.

Here's an important principle: The radical difference between love and sex is, if you love someone, you want the best for him or her. Radical respect means putting the needs of others above our own desires. Jason didn't have sex with Jennifer because he knew it was not best in the long run for Jennifer. He had the intelligence to realize that although they really liked each other, there was a good chance they would not get married. Radical respect means looking out for the other's interest above your own. Here's what Paul had to say:

Do nothing out of selfish ambition or vain conceit, but in humility consider others better than yourselves. Each of you should look not only to your own interests, but also to the interests of others. Your attitude should be the same as that of Christ Jesus. (Philippians 2:3–5)

It's pretty clear—the Christian approach to dating is radically different.

Some people reading this may believe the same as the eighteen-year-old sexually active friend of mine who exclaimed, "God is a total killjoy when it comes to sex." I don't think so. Although the Bible is definitely not a sex manual, I believe its words and values clearly have our best interest in view.

What the Bible Says About . . .

Adultery

You shall not commit adultery. (Exodus 20:14)

Adultery is when two people have sexual intercourse and at least one of them is married to someone else. To put it simply, adultery tears lives apart and usually causes an incredible amount of turmoil, not only for the couple, but for the others involved. Cathy and I have friends who have broken up their marriages because of adulterous affairs, and it has *never* been easy. Relationships are broken and pain is the result. When God tells us in the Ten Commandments, "You shall not commit adultery," He surely is not the great killjoy. He simply wants the best for us.

Fornication

It is God's will that you should be sanctified: that you should avoid sexual immorality. (1 Thessalonians 4:3)

Fornication is when two people have a sexual experience and neither is married. Again, I believe it's pretty evident that God wants the best for us, and that's why He commands us to flee from immorality and fornication. I often have the privilege of performing wedding ceremonies of people close to me. In my premarital counseling sessions I always ask the question, "What kind of baggage are you bringing into this relationship?" I'm referring to a dysfunctional family, alcoholism, sexual abuse, or other issues of trauma. Almost always the first answer is, "Well, I was in this other relationship, and we went too far physically." Please remember, there are consequences to our sexual actions. It's true God forgives us, but most people who are sexually active before marriage still feel the consequences. The best way to keep from suffering the consequences of a premarital sexual relationship is to take this command from God seriously and obey God's Word. Flee from fornication!

One Flesh

> *Haven't you read . . . that at the beginning the Creator "made them male and female," and said, "For this reason a man will leave his father and mother and be united to his wife, and the two will become one flesh"? So they are no longer two, but one. Therefore what God has joined together, let man not separate.* (Matthew 19:4–6)

This is a noteworthy quote from the lips of Jesus. When a man and a woman come together sexually, two become one! The very act of intercourse is a perfect illustration of two becoming one. Today, one of the major philosophies being touted is that casual sex is okay. I honestly don't believe in casual sex. How can two people become one and call that "casual"?

The Answer: Radical Respect

> *Flee from sexual immorality. All other sins a man commits are*
> *outside his body, but he who sins sexually sins against his own body.*
> (1 Corinthians 6:18)

We are challenged in this passage to flee, or run, from sexual immorality. Verse 18 apparently tells us that sin is sin, but that sexual sin is against our own bodies. When we sin against our bodies, the temples of God, it tends to stay with us longer psychologically and emotionally. Frankly, I know people who made negative decisions in junior high and high school who are now middle-aged and are still dealing with the sexual sins of their teenage years. I'm not talking just about people who got pregnant. I'm talking about people's emotions and feelings being paralyzed because of past experiences. They feel guilty, embarrassed, and sometimes even unworthy of enjoying sex with their spouse.

> *Do you not know that your body is a temple of the Holy Spirit,*
> *who is in you, whom you have received from God? You are not your*
> *own; you were bought at a price. Therefore honor God with your body.*
> (1 Corinthians 6:19–20)

Because our bodies are the temples of God through the Holy Spirit, we *must* treat each other with the utmost respect. To treat one another as a temple of God means to treat the other person with honor. Jason treated Jennifer with respect because of his commitment to God.

To look at this passage another way, we understand that Jesus Christ gave His body for us on the cross. Now as Christians, our response to the cross is to give our bodies to God. One of the most important elements of being a follower of Jesus Christ is to honor and obey Him by giving Him your body. Paul put it this way:

> *Therefore, I urge you, brothers, in view of God's mercy, to offer your bodies as living sacrifices, holy and pleasing to God—this is your spiritual act of worship.* (Romans 12:1)

God doesn't want to kill our joy when it comes to sexuality. He created sex. It's His idea. He wants the best for us, and His challenge to every Christian is that of "radical respect."

Things to Think About

1. Radical respect is definitely a different philosophy from what you hear about in the secular world. What do you see as the differences?
2. Our bodies are the temples of the Holy Spirit. How does this principle affect your relationship with people of the opposite sex?
3. What are specific, practical ways you can "outdo one another in showing honor" in a dating relationship?
4. Do you view the radical respect philosophy as one of many options for Christian dating or the only option for a Christ-centered relationship?

Respect Builders

1. Watch your language! A great respect builder is to watch how you talk about people of the opposite sex (and the same sex, for that matter). When you are talking about a person being "easy"

sexually or describing his or her body in sexual terms, you are talking about a child of God, created in His image. Christians are challenged to *love* and *encourage* each other with our lives and with our words. The next time you are ready to make a sexual joke or innuendo, hold your tongue!

2. Treat each person you know as a child of God. Read Matthew 25:34–40. This passage is about meeting the needs of the poor and oppressed. Look at verse 40 and write out how this verse especially relates to the radical respect concept.

Team Effort

Radical respect:

Below are listed several situations. Write out and then discuss with your group or family how you would apply radical respect to each situation:

1. Listening to other students talk in sexual innuendoes to a girl or guy on campus;
2. Going further on a date than you feel is right before God;
3. Taking a date to a sexually explicit movie;
4. Dating a non-Christian;
5. Kissing, fondling, oral sex.

Chapter Twelve

Dating

As a youth pastor, I could always tell when the high-school prom was about to take place. Many of the girls in my youth group would begin to feel extremely depressed. It's the Sunday before the big dance and it looks like they'll be spending another prom night at the movies with their girl friends, who also weren't asked to the prom. To tell you the truth, I started to resent proms because of all the damage they did to the self-images and emotions of my young friends. It is a shame that an event that draws only about 25 percent of the school's population can do so much damage to so many of those not attending.

This emphasis on the prom brings into focus the fact that a great American institution—The Date—is going as strong as ever. For many of us, dating is a huge paradox. Most people dream of the perfect romantic date, and many teens can hardly wait to start dating. Dating can be really fun. It can be all you ever dreamed about. But the paradox is that dating can also cause more distress, hurt feelings, and self-doubt than just about anything else I've ever seen. Before we deal with some helpful advice, I want to clear up two misunderstandings about dating.

Misunderstanding 1: Everybody dates in high school.

Wrong. Statistics tell us that 50 percent of the girls and 40 percent of the guys graduating from high school have *never* dated. If you happen to fall into this category, you are definitely not alone. Here's a note that a youth volunteer wrote on the back of a church bulletin and gave to me one time after I shared this statistic at a youth meeting: "Thanks, Jim, for letting our kids know that not everyone dates in high school. I believed the biggest problem in my life was that I didn't date in high school. I thought I was the only one. I hated myself, my looks, my personality, my church—everything. Years later, I realized how grateful I was for being a 'late bloomer.' I was able to establish positive high-school friendships that have lasted a lifetime, and I have a wonderful husband I met while in college. I wish I'd heard your talk years ago."

Here's an excerpt from another letter that has a different perspective on the same issue: "I wish I hadn't dated at such a young age. I didn't know how to handle my emotions. I let guys use me. Of course I wasn't aware of this at the time. But now, after two abortions, I wish I hadn't grown up so fast."

Misunderstanding 2: If you want to be popular, you've got to have sex.

Again, this is simply wrong. *Everybody isn't doing it!* If you could survey some of the most talented and popular people at your school, you would find out that not everyone is sexually active. Yes, they have a normal sex drive and curiosity and all the rest, but they recognize that they must deal with other more important priorities.

One of the finest compliments I've ever heard was a statement by a young girl in our youth group. She was telling me about one of our high-school seniors whom she described in this way: "John is cute, he is popular at school, and he's so involved in sports. I love being around him because he's so together, and if you can believe this, he is still a virgin!"

I think my young friend was amazed that a person could be cute, popular, and "together" and still *choose* purity. Thousands of people have chosen as an act of their wills *not* to be sexually active and still seem to have a lot of friends and a certain degree of popularity.

A few things I've said are worth repeating. First, it isn't true that everybody dates in high school. Second, it isn't necessary to be sexually active to be popular. Dating can be fun—and your time for dating will come. Whether that time is now or in the future, I have some suggestions for you.

Dating Suggestions

Establish a Friendship

As I shared earlier, the first day I saw the woman who is now my wife, I fell deeply "in infatuation" with her. She didn't know I existed, but I knew it was "infatuation at first sight." Back then, I might have said "*love* at first sight," but now I know better. Anyway, I'll never forget that day in the campus gym.

I was at freshman orientation with two other newcomers to the college whom I had met at dinner. Cathy was being entertained by a group of upperclassmen who seemed to have some of the same feelings

I had! I leaned over to my two freshman friends, pointed out Cathy to them, and said, "See that girl over there? I'm going to take her out sometime." They looked at her and her beauty, they looked at me, and they laughed. They thought I was kidding, but I wasn't.

I was lucky enough to have the same English class and psychology class Cathy had. I would try to sit next to her whenever I could manage it—which was pretty often, because I would wait for her to come in before I would sit down.

Well, to make a long story short, we became "just friends." Cathy had another boyfriend, and she would even tell me about their dates. But you know what? By becoming "just friends" we established a brother/sister relationship that served as a solid foundation between us. We spent a large amount of time talking and becoming closer friends. We had a great deal of fun together long before we became boyfriend and girlfriend.

I think that's why we still like being together. We started off as friends rather than lovers. Far too often, though, people in a dating relationship do not work on establishing a friendship. That's why some relationships develop many hurt feelings and misunderstandings.

Avoid Isolation

Another factor to consider in a dating relationship is to avoid isolating yourself. If you spend time only with your boyfriend or girlfriend and you have little time with your own friends, you probably have a poor relationship.

Often the following imaginary scene happens in real life: Boy and girl meet. They like each other very much. They spend more time with each other. They come to enjoy each other's company so much that they begin to exclude their other friends. Finally, they spend little or no time with anyone else. Their friends complain, but to no avail. Boy and girl become sexually involved. They break up. Both are feeling the heartbreak. Both feel like they've lost their other friends too, and that they have no one to turn to in their loneliness.

In a positive dating relationship, even when people are "going together," they must maintain old friendships and spend time with other people. A positive relationship does not involve complete dependency; it involves a mutual love and respect that says, "I love you so much that I'm willing to share you with your friends."

Don't Stay Together Only for Security

One of the most difficult things to do in life is to break off a relationship, yet often it must be done. Most teenage relationships go on too long to be truly healthy. Then when they end, the emotional trauma cuts deep. Often one or both partners will attempt to restore the relationship. But there is nothing worse than trying to put back together something that should not be put back together. If you are hanging on to a relationship simply for the security it offers, muster up all your courage and break it off. The sooner you break up, the easier it will be.

Sometimes we don't know how to act around a person with whom we have ended a relationship. For some people, it is possible to continue to be friends. It might take time, but try to maintain a friendship. To do this, you'll have to stay away from gossiping or telling negative stories about your "ex." Try to put your differences aside and work at developing a brother/sister relationship. If you feel that a friendship with your ex is impossible, that's okay too. Sometimes when a serious relationship ends, the only way for the people involved to heal and move on is to let go of each other completely.

Plan Fun and Enjoyable Dates

The average American date seems to consist of dinner, a movie, and making out. I'm sure I'm exaggerating—but only a little! Because the purpose of dating is to become better friends, it's important to plan dates that will help you really get to know each other. Many dates are boring because people do the same thing at the same time at the same place. Sameness can cause even a good relationship to go sour, so be creative with your dates.

In case you don't feel creative, here are more than seventy creative and not-so-creative date suggestions. I've compiled these through the years in brainstorming sessions with high schoolers and by reading a couple of helpful books. Read through the list, think of other ideas on your own, and be creative with your dating life!

Active Dates/Sports

- Ride bikes or a bicycle built for two
- Visit a beach or lake
- Ice-skate
- Shop
- Play video games
- Canoe
- Go horseback riding
- Go hiking or climbing
- Dance
- Play pinball or miniature golf

- Play croquet
- Water-ski
- Go bowling
- Try creative writing (poems, short stories)
- Take photos together
- Play Ping-Pong
- Play board games or card games
- Plant a garden
- Wash your cars
- Read a book aloud
- Do homework together
- Collect something
- Take a walk
- Play tennis
- Play chess
- Sail
- Fly kites
- Fish
- Ride a ferry
- Attend a Bible study
- Snow-ski
- Jog
- Make something together (try one of those paint-your-own-ceramics shops, for example!)
- Go on a scavenger hunt
- Go rafting or tubing on a river
- Build a tree house

Food

- Go out to dinner—casual or fancy
- Share a pizza and talk
- Have a barbecue
- Go on a picnic
- Cook dinner for your parents
- Take a frozen yogurt break and talk
- "Kidnap" the other person for breakfast
- Cook dinner together
- Bake cookies
- Make homemade ice cream

Spectator

- Attend a play
- Go to the movies
- Go to a school function
- Enjoy parties and friends
- Go to a sports event
- Feed the birds at your local park
- Watch TV at someone's house
- Go to a concert
- Attend a Bible study
- Watch hang gliders
- Go to a public lecture

Places to Go

- The mountains in summer to hike or bike
- An interesting historical site
- The circus
- The mountains in winter to play in the snow and build snow people
- An observatory
- The county fair
- Museums
- The zoo
- The park to swing
- Church and youth group functions

Serve Others

- Have a Bible study
- Work at church together
- Do volunteer work together

Remember That Dating Is Preparation for Marriage

Not every person you date will be someone you would want to marry, but most of the people you date will become someone's marriage partner. That's why dating is good preparation for marriage. I think you should treat each date as a special date. By dating, you can learn a lot about the kind of person you would like to marry. As you date different people, you will get a better view of what you want in a wife or husband.

At times it frightens me when two people who have dated only each other plan to get married. Most people need to experience a variety of relationships before they settle down for that one special lifelong relationship. Listen to what a friend of mine told me recently: "I knew I loved Karen, but I never realized how much until one summer in college when we decided to date others. And, you know, that time really helped me see what it was I liked about Karen, and it only convinced me more that I was in love with her."

Another real benefit of dating is that you get a better idea of how you relate to the opposite sex in various situations. It can teach you some important things about yourself and about getting along with another person. And these lessons will help you be more sensitive and act more appropriately when you are ready to settle down and get married.

One last thought before we move on. Because each person you date is created by God and loved by our Lord, you should treat him or her with the same respect, dignity, and kindness you want to receive from others.

Avoid Getting Too Close Too Soon

Several years ago my friend Mike Yaconelli gave me something to think about. He'd spent many years working with young people and seemed to understand them better than most anyone I know. He said, "Today it seems that too many kids take breaking up with a boyfriend or girlfriend way too hard. Their grief is almost as if they were married and going through a divorce." He then made this crushing statement: "I think it's because too many young people are having sex so soon after they meet that they are dealing with a deeper kind of intimacy than young people were even a few years ago."

You know what? Mike was—and still is—right. Kids are becoming intimate so soon in their relationships that it is taking a terrible toll on their emotional health. Consider the following scenario.

Tim and Sara like each other. In fact, they think they love each other. They hadn't meant to get so deeply involved physically, but they have. Call it curiosity, lust, sex drive, or just enjoying each other's touch. Whatever you call it, now they're in trouble. They've been intimate, but neither one is emotionally able to handle the deep commitment that goes with physical intimacy. The relationship begins to deteriorate until finally they break it off. It's too bad, because they might have become a great couple. Instead, they must suffer the painful emotional consequences that come with breaking off physical intimacy.

If you have or would like to have a special relationship, move very slowly. That special friendship is worth the wait, and the slower pace could possibly be one of the wisest decisions you will ever make. No one I've ever met who has waited to get physical in a relationship has ever regretted waiting. Think about that statement for a minute. I surely can't say the same about the number of my friends who didn't wait.

Advice on Dating Non-Christians

Now for the big question: Should Christians date non-Christians? Every time I speak at a conference, every time I give a talk related to sex, and any time the subject of dating comes up, I am asked for my opinion on Christians dating non-Christians. Here it is.

Contrary to the belief of some people, not all non-Christians are interested in getting into bed on the first date. Not all non-Christians are pot smokers or heavy drinkers. I know many fine non-Christians.

Some of the kindest, gentlest, most talented people I know do not profess faith in the Lord Jesus Christ. I think it is a shame that well-meaning Christians give us advice that seems to say, "Stay away from non-Christian pagans. They'll only pull you down!" It seems to me that Jesus said something about us Christians being the salt of the earth and the light of the world (see Matthew 5:13–14). Jesus spent time with sinners and helped them understand the real meaning of life. I think, then, that a Christian should be able to name some close non-Christian friends. I hope you are cultivating deep relationships with Christians and non-Christians alike.

I don't, however, believe in what some people call "missionary dating"—that is, dating a non-Christian to make him or her a Christian. Once in a great while this plan works, but most often it leads to hurt, rejection, and misunderstanding, and at times a real falling away from God. Although I believe we all need to have non-Christian friends, I'm afraid that when a Christian and non-Christian date, it is similar to mixing apples and oranges.

Let me explain: No verses in the Bible say, "Thou shalt not date nonbelievers." Clear-cut guidelines, however, tell us we should not *marry* nonbelievers. Guess what? Dating leads to marriage.

I've seen too many relationships end in disaster when one person was a Christian and the other wasn't. I'm sure you've heard the sad stories also. Guy meets girl; they fall in love. Guy falls away from God because his new "god" is his girlfriend. Or guy meets girl and they fall in love. Guy and girl get married. Girl is a Christian, he is not. Girl grows in one direction with one set of goals and standards while guy grows in the opposite direction with conflicting goals and standards. Guy and girl divorce with much heartbreak. I would imagine that when the apostle Paul advised against being yoked together with unbelievers (2 Corinthians 6:14), he was writing from his own experience of watching the heartache and confusion of "unequally yoked" (KJV) or "mismated" (RSV) people trying to have good marriages.

A friend of mine once gave what I think to be very sound advice: "Human beings are composed of body, soul and spirit. When a Christian marries a non-Christian, the most they can have is two-thirds of a relationship." I would simply add this: If you date non-Christians, you are playing with fire, and not for the reason that they'll take you straight to hell. You are playing with fire because, while you may be very much alike, you are very different at the same time. Also, why settle for second best when you can have God's best in your life?

At this point, you might be objecting because I keep talking about marriage. You might even be saying, "There aren't any Christian guys or girls around here for me to date." Here's the straight scoop: If you usually date non-Christians, then chances are you will marry a non-Christian. As I've said, the Bible is very clear when it comes to believers marrying non-Christians: "Do not be mismated with unbelievers. For what partnership have righteousness and iniquity? Or what fellowship has light with darkness?" (2 Corinthians 6:14 RSV). Two people having two separate sets of goals and two separate "lords" will have a difficult time ever really coming together and developing a strong marriage.

My goal in this chapter has been to get you to think about what is best for you and your relationship with God. I caution you to think through your dating relationships seriously. It could mean the difference between a happy, fulfilled future and a future of disappointment and painful consequences. When it comes to dating, don't settle for second best!

Things to Think About

1. What advice would you give a person who is ready to date but is not being asked out?
2. Which suggestions on dating found in this chapter are most helpful for you? Why?
3. Name two or three date ideas from the list in this chapter that appeal to you and that cost little or nothing.
4. What is your opinion about dating non-Christians? On what facts and experiences is your opinion based?

Respect Builders

1. Make your own list of creative, fun, and enjoyable dates. You might even want to arrange your creative ideas into categories:

   - Least expensive dates
   - Most outrageous dates
   - First dates
   - Group dates

2. Avoid dating non-Christians. When you put this statement in black and white, it sounds harsh. But remember, you are not being urged to avoid *friendships* with non-Christians. God loves them, and He wants to love them through you. But dating is a very special kind of relationship—and evidence shows that it can lead to marriage!

   If you're not sure what the Bible says about marrying non-Christians, read 2 Corinthians 6:14. Based on this verse, what are some reasons for not marrying a person who isn't a Christian?

Team Effort

How Christians are to treat each other:

Review Ephesians 4 and 5. These chapters talk about unity among believers and about how Christians are to live. The passage culminates with a beautiful description of Christian marriage. And remember while you're reading this that everything Scripture says about how Christians in general are to treat each other applies to Christian marriage partners (and dating as well)!

In the following chart, list instructions from Ephesians 4 and 5 for how Christians are to treat each other. (I've given you a running start.)

How Christians Are to Treat Each Other
Humbly
Gently

Chapter Thirteen

Parties

When the phone rang, it was Jill's mother. (Jill was a sixteen-year-old in my youth group.) As I talked to her on the phone, Jill's mother seemed a little pushy and a little desperate. She told me that recently Jill had "really changed for the worse." Jill was partying all the time, was losing interest in school, and had a bad attitude around the house. Her mother said that I had to help her wayward daughter and asked when I could meet with her.

It usually takes a while to get going in a counseling session. When a parent makes the appointment, the young person rarely wants to see me if he or she doesn't know me, and often he or she expects me to side with the parents—which I don't always do! But Jill and I hit it off almost immediately. She confided that she had been apprehensive about meeting me, and I confided that I'd been apprehensive about meeting her too!

After all the terrible things her mother had said, I couldn't believe this was her daughter! Jill was open, honest, polite, and very friendly.

This told me that although she might have a bad attitude at home, she had a lot going for her. I could tell that Jill had as much potential as anyone I had recently met.

We met together a couple of times. Her story was similar to hundreds and hundreds of others. Yes, she was partying too much. Yes, she had experimented with drugs and alcohol. Yes, she was having trouble in school, and it was also true that things weren't going well at home. Tension was in the air—but it wasn't all from Jill. Her parents were experiencing a lot of stress at work and in their relationship with each other.

Despite this rather difficult situation, one thing in Jill's favor was that she said she was a Christian. In her words, "I'm not much of a Christian, but I do believe and I really want to grow in my faith." I believed her. I believed that she was sincere, and I asked one of our female advisers to spend some time with her on a one-to-one basis. They went shopping, played a little tennis, and even started doing a weekly Bible study together.

It seemed as though things were going much better for Jill. Then late one night, I got a call from her. She had been to a party, and she was very drunk and needed a ride home. My wife and I got out of bed and went to pick her up. By that time, she had sobered up enough to talk sense, and she definitely needed to talk about things. She had not partied as much lately as she had before, but tonight's party had been important. Most of her friends had planned to attend, and a guy she really liked had kept asking if she was going to be there. He paid a lot of attention to her that night. They drank too much and Jill had blacked out. She was now sobbing in our car: "I think we went all the way, but I don't even remember." Jill was stunned, shocked at herself, and very depressed.

One day in my office a few months after what Jill called "the worst night in my life," we were talking about the need to discuss the topic of partying in our youth group. Jill and I came up with these five suggestions, which we titled "Practical Guidelines for Partying." Take the time to read this list. Learn from Jill's experience! Don't wait to learn some of these lessons from personal heartbreak.

Practical Guidelines for Partying

If Partying Is a Weak Point in Your Life, Don't Go to Parties

If you enjoy going to parties but you can't seem to control your actions as you would like, don't go. It's not worth the pain, hurt, and temptation you might subject yourself to. Remember that we must live with our choices and our consequences, so choose—an act of your will!—not to go. Also, I think it is important to replace your old negative actions with new positive actions. If, for example, you have been a heavy partier and you want to stop, then don't just spend time watching TV and doing nothing. Replace the time you spent partying with other more positive activities.

The key word here is "replace." It is much easier to overcome a bad habit or weakness in your life when you replace the negative experience with a positive one. My suggestion is that you write down on a piece of paper alternatives to partying that you would enjoy. Then when the temptation comes and you don't think you can handle the pressure, you can look at other possible options and choose one of those more positive experiences. As a reference point, the preceding chapter has a solid list of date ideas that could be done with your boyfriend or girlfriend, or even a group of buddies.

Host "Clean" Parties

It is not necessarily wrong to go to a party. Not all parties will bring you down. To party really means to celebrate—and Christians have more to celebrate than anyone I know. Jill suggested that some of the Christians she knew could host what she called "clean" parties. The great thing about a party is spending time with people. Instead of going to parties where you have no control over what will take place, host parties that will be great fun and at the same time will keep you from getting into trouble.

As a Christian, if You Go to Parties, Invite the Lord Jesus to Go With You

Does that sound corny? It shouldn't. If you are a Christian, Jesus wants to be involved in everything in which you are involved. If you actively invite Christ to attend a party with you, this awareness of Him will help you refrain from doing things that might disappoint both you and God. Also, you might be surprised to find that you have a better time than you've ever had!

Choose Friends Who Will Help You Be the Best Person You Can Possibly Be

Jill had to take a serious look at the friends with whom she was spending most of her time. She finally decided that many of her problems stemmed from the kind of people she had been hanging around with. At first, she didn't think they were affecting her lifestyle, but when she really thought about it, she realized that she had been compromising many of her beliefs because of peer pressure. Jill decided to choose close friends who would be a better influence on her and whose lifestyle would challenge her to live a more fulfilled life.

Christians Do Not Live by the World's Standards

Jill asked me to add this guideline to the list. Her point is an important one, and perhaps Jesus said it best: "No one can serve two masters. Either he will hate the one and love the other, or he will be devoted to the one and despise the other" (Matthew 6:24). Most of us want to "have our cake and eat it too." If we are honest, we all have times when we want to live by the world's standards and also by God's standards. Sometimes we have to decide which is the very best standard to live by, and then go for it. Jill looked at and experienced what the world could offer and what God could offer, and she chose God. She told me not long ago, "Not for one moment have I regretted my choice."

When God's standards seem rather abstract to us, that is when we need to turn to the Bible. I can think of several paragraphs written by Paul that set forth God's standards for us. These paragraphs really challenged me as a high-school student, and they still challenge me today. I encourage you to take the time to read and study Colossians 3:1–17.

Arguing that because "you have been raised with Christ," Paul urges you to "set your hearts on things above, where Christ is seated at the right hand of God. Set your minds on things above, not on earthly things" (vv. 1–2). As he continues, Paul spares no words as he exhorts us, "Put to death, therefore, whatever belongs to your earthly nature" and "put on the new self, which is being renewed in knowledge in the image of its Creator" (vv. 5, 10). Paul then offers us some specific instructions:

> *Therefore, as God's chosen people, holy and dearly loved, clothe yourselves with compassion, kindness, humility, gentleness and patience.*

Bear with each other and forgive whatever grievances you may have against one another. Forgive as the Lord forgave you. And over all these virtues put on love, which binds them all together in perfect unity. (vv. 12–14)

Take time to read and study the Colossians passage in its entirety. Paul clearly defines the high standards we Christians should aim for in our daily lives. These standards should apply to our behavior at parties as much as they should apply to any aspect of our lives. Let me echo Paul as I close the chapter: Choose friends and activities that honor God, don't invite temptation into your life by going to parties that you know you shouldn't, and trust God to be with you through whatever temptations might still arise.

Things to Think About

1. Do you think Christians should attend parties that offer drugs or drinking? Why or why not?
2. What are the pros and cons of attending parties?
3. What are some alternative ideas for things to do instead of partying?
4. In Colossians 3:1 (quoted in this chapter), Paul tells Christians to "set your hearts on things above." What do you think that means?

Respect Builders

1. If partying is a weak point in your life, don't go to parties. List at least ten things you could do instead of going to a party. (See chapter 12 on dating if you need some ideas.)

2. Host "clean" parties. Write a complete plan for a "clean" party you and your friends would enjoy. You might want to decide on a theme. Describe the decorations, the refreshments, and the activities. Make a list of the people you would like to invite to your party.

- Theme
- Decorations
- Refreshments
- Guests
- Date and Time

Now clear it with your parents and do it!

Team Effort

Remember that Christians do not live by the world's standards:

Think back to the last party you attended. What sort of standards did people seem to be following? How were these standards and behaviors similar to what God calls us to follow? How were these standards and behaviors different from what God wants our lives to be like?

Summarize your observations and ideas on the following chart and discuss them.

Standards at the Party	God's Standards

Chapter Fourteen

Drugs and Drinking

I'm no prude. In fact, many adults who read this book might think I should be a little more prudish. But I'll be honest with you: Drugs and drinking scare me. Maybe it's because I've seen too many of the negative side effects of drinking in my own family. Maybe it's Steven, whom I met a few years ago. At seventeen, his brain was fried from putting too many drugs into his body—and he had once had all the potential in the world for leading a happy and fulfilled life. Maybe it's Jill, who got drunk and now isn't sure if she is a virgin or not. The list could go on; the stories only get worse, especially when you consider that most of the deaths in automobile accidents are caused by drunk drivers or that over 60 percent of rapes involve alcohol or drug abuse.

I'm especially frightened when it comes to drugs like ecstasy (also called "E," among other things) and crystal meth, which are ruining the lives of not just teens, but entire communities across this country. I hope you never even experiment with drugs or alcohol. The odds are that by the time you are eighteen, you will have already tried one, if not both. I'm not going to tell you that every time you drink or take drugs horrible things will happen to you, because they won't. But these substances present an incredibly powerful danger that can irreversibly damage your mind, body, and spirit. Because there is alcoholism in my family system, I choose not to drink. I believe there is a biological predisposition toward alcoholism and have seen too many lives and relationships ruined because of addictions.

Consider This . . .

Think Through Your Actions: Who's in Control?

A person who is drunk or high is not in control of his or her actions. Charlie Shedd has now passed away, but he was a mentor in my life. I remember him saying that it is a good idea where sex is involved to keep checking who's in control. Are you doing the thinking or is somebody else doing it for you? Do you really want to do this? Or are you doing it because somebody else is pressuring you? I've heard far too many stories about people who got drunk or high, couldn't control their actions, and bingo, a pregnancy occurred—bringing with it all the lifelong effects that come with unwanted pregnancies.

If You Drink, Don't Drive; If You Take Drugs, Don't Drive

I have a name for people who drink and drive: FOOLS.

Science has proven that even one beer can keep some people from being in control of their driving. A drunk driver (and I'm not necessarily talking about the kind of drunk we see in the movies) is not only a dangerous weapon who may kill or maim himself or herself; a drunk driver has the definite ability to kill or maim innocent bystanders too. If you drink or take drugs, don't drive.

Many years ago I watched a movie about a "happy drunk" named *Arthur*. To be honest, it depressed me greatly. Most drunks aren't *that* happy or *that* funny. Furthermore, most drunk drivers aren't as lucky as Arthur was when he drove through downtown New York City, barely missing other cars and pedestrians. *Arthur* was a make-believe story. If you want the real story, read your newspaper. Drunk-driving accidents happen every day, and most of the time they don't have happy endings.

Many movies, TV shows, and tabloids depict celebrities' wild party lifestyle, but too many times these celebrities are glamorized with their partying escapades. In recent years people like Paris Hilton, Britney Spears, and Lindsay Lohan have dominated teen magazines with their intoxicated nights out partying around the world. Frankly, my heart breaks for those girls and the pain their lifestyles have caused them. Basically they are wonderfully talented young women who didn't handle their drug and alcohol use very well. I hope the best for them, but I also hope you never are tempted to experiment with a life that looks good on the outside but is incredibly painful on the inside.

Alcoholism Is on the Rise

Fifteen percent of today's teenagers are alcoholics. More than three million teenagers in the United States today are problem drinkers! They don't look or act like the stereotypical alcoholic. (Few people do!) They are addicted for life to something that has broken up more homes and ruined more lives than anything in the world. If you have even the slightest suspicion that you could possibly be an alcoholic, get help now. Don't wait until you hurt your family or ruin your life. Also, if you want to have an eye-opening experience, visit a local chapter of Alcoholics Anonymous (AA). You'll see very quickly that alcoholics are not happy people until they become recovered alcoholics; even then, many carry the scars of alcoholism for life.

The Bible says, "Don't drink too much wine, for many evils lie along that path; be filled instead with the Holy Spirit, and controlled by him" (Ephesians 5:18 TLB). I wish the Bible said, "Don't drink or take drugs; they will ruin your life!" But it doesn't. It simply says that we shouldn't get drunk (or high), but that we should be filled instead with the Holy Spirit. When you are intoxicated, you definitely cannot be allowing the Holy Spirit of God to work in your life.

I know a person who chose not to drink, even though most of his friends and family drank. Some of his very close loved ones were alcoholics. I asked him once, "Why don't you drink?" I will never forget his answer: "I love the taste of some types of alcohol, and there is nothing better on a hot day than a cold glass of beer. *But I've decided I don't need it.* I'm not pushing my opinion on others, because I'm not convinced that everyone shouldn't drink; but let me tell you why I don't drink or take drugs. I could drink just one beer a week and see nothing wrong with it except that my alcoholic father would see that one beer and use it to justify his *case* of beer. I don't want to have a silent negative witness to my friends or family. And besides all that, I don't need to drink or take drugs to be accepted. I'd rather be in control of my mind, spirit, and body at all times."

All I can add to this statement is, "Well said, my friend; I can't think of anyone who wouldn't respect your position."

Drugs

I get nervous about any mood-altering substance. Too many times I've seen my friends innocently get involved with pot and as a result have their brains "fried" on acid (LSD), shrooms, and E. This doesn't mean that everyone who has ever experimented with marijuana will end up passed out in the back of some alley with needle marks up and down his or her arms. Anyone who becomes involved with any mood-altering substance, however, must carefully and logically think through his or her actions.

Here's the straight scoop. Drugs work! They can make you feel good and they *will* get you high every single time. Here's the problem: Because drugs alter your mood, a person can easily become dependent on them. The fact is that young people who take drugs at an early age often quit coping with stress in a normal way and become dependent on drugs to make them feel better. After a while, people become preoccupied with getting high because it is the only way they can function. And most of the people who are preoccupied with getting high are not the skid-row bums. They are the people who have normal jobs and semi-normal families. Yet if you watch them over the years, they bring a great deal of tragedy into their own lives.

I must discuss one more important issue. I was speaking recently at a high school, and I said to the students: "There is great evidence today that there is a biological predisposition to the disease of alcoholism.[1] This means alcoholism can be inherited from your family. So if your dad, mom, brothers, sisters, aunts, uncles, or grandparents are alcoholics, you have a much greater risk of becoming an alcoholic. Your body will crave alcohol differently from other people."

After the assembly, a young man walked up to me and said, "What you are telling me is that if my dad is an alcoholic, then I'm at greater risk to become an alcoholic and I shouldn't drink."

I nodded my head. "Yes, that's pretty much what I'm trying to get across."

He said, "That's not fair!"

I replied, "Who said anything about life being fair?"

As we continued to talk, I assessed that the young man was already a budding alcoholic. He told me he could drink five cans of beer and not get drunk. Then he added, "But you probably don't believe that."

I smiled and said, "No, I absolutely believe you, and that proves my point that you are most probably already an alcoholic." He looked at me, confused. I went on, "Alcoholics have a very *high tolerance* for alcohol consumption. You can drink differently from your friends because your body is addicted to alcohol. People with a high tolerance for alcohol, people who can 'hold their liquor,' simply drink under their tolerance level. But eventually their bodies will break down and their tolerance levels will change, or they will drink over their tolerance level and major problems will occur."

My friend shook my hand, gave me an understanding look, and walked away. I hope he quits drinking, or he will find himself being one more negative statistic.

My cry to students today is, *Reconsider your drinking or drug habits.* I choose not to have even one drink and, of course, no drugs. I can only say that anyone who takes on a lifestyle of abstinence from drugs or alcohol will never, never regret it. For the drinkers and drug users who suffer from out-of-control decisions, regret is probably one of the dominant themes of their lives. Think about it.

Things to Think About

1. Why do you think some young people drink enough to get drunk?

2. Are most teenagers able to control their drinking and drugs? Why or why not?

3. Which philosophy of drinking do you feel closest to at this time of your life:

   ☐ Never touch the stuff!

   ☐ People can drink but not in excess.

   ☐ It's a free country; people have the right to drink as much as they want.

4. Without mentioning names, do you know of anyone who has had a negative experience with drugs or drinking? How has this affected your own thoughts about using drugs or alcohol?

5. Do you think smoking marijuana is more harmful or less harmful than drinking alcohol? Why?

Respect Builders

1. Think through your actions and realize who is in control.
   - Can you be completely in control when you drink or take drugs?
   - What are some disadvantages or dangers of being out of control?
   - Read Ephesians 5:18. What does this verse mean?

2. If you drink, don't drive; if you take drugs, don't drive. List some guidelines you might need to follow if you drink or take drugs and then realize you should not drive.

The guidelines you just wrote down also apply if you are a passenger and the driver of the car starts drinking or taking drugs. Do not ride with this person. Make sure you have an alternative plan. Write down that alternative plan.

3. Tennis star Venus Williams made an anti-drug commercial in which she states, "Drugs kill dreams." Do you think this is true? Why or why not?

Team Effort

The "Just Say No" game is an excellent way to help you practice saying no to drugs.

The "Just Say No" Game[2]

The object of the game is to respond to a high-pressure situation in such a way that those applying pressure will back off. Try to develop several creative ways to say no by acting out the following situations. Vote for the best responses.

Drug Offers

1. You are at school in between classes, and someone asks you to walk into the bathroom to smoke pot.
2. A boy you know says he snuck two of his mother's prescription pain-killers out of the medicine cabinet and asks you to meet him after school to share them.
3. One of the high-school seniors offers to give you a ride home and tells you he has some pure meth and wants you to smoke it with him.

4. At one of the local hangouts, a girl offers you a pink pill and promises it will make you feel as though you are in another world.

5. You see a friend under the football stadium, shooting something into his arm. He offers to let you try it for free.

Alcohol Offers

1. Your older brother and his friend pick you up from a party, and his friend offers you a cold beer for the trip home.

2. At a party, some kids get into the parents' liquor cabinet. Everyone starts drinking out of the bottle of vodka.

3. Your parents take you out to a nice dinner at a local club. Your dad orders something to drink for everyone and tells you it is okay for you to have one.

4. On the drive home from school, one of the people you consider to be your friend pulls out a bottle of champagne and pops the cork, asking you to drink up.

5. On a fishing trip, you go up the river with your brother. You are in the middle of the forest and he says that because no one is around, you can have a beer.

Chapter Fifteen

Guilt and Forgiveness

We used to have a dog named Buffy whose favorite meals as a puppy were flowers, curtains, and tennis shoes. Every day my wife, Cathy, and I would yell at Buffy and threaten her within an inch of her life. But it didn't seem to help much. She just kept chewing on anything and everything.

Here's a funny thing about Buffy, though. She almost seemed to *know* when she was doing something wrong. As soon as she tore up my newest jogging shoes or ate all the daisies Cathy put on the coffee table, she would run and hide under the kitchen table. And there she sat looking as innocent as she could, trying to pretend nothing had happened.

But Cathy and I were wise to Buffy. We knew that if the dog was under the kitchen table, it meant that she had been up to no good. Sure enough, we wouldn't have to look very hard to find evidence of Buffy's most recent mischief. We human beings are a lot like Buffy.

We do wrong things, and then we feel guilty for what we've done. We have guilty consciences.

Dr. James Dobson tells about a poll in which kids were asked, "What is conscience?" One six-year-old girl said a conscience is the spot inside that "burns if you're not good." A six-year-old boy said he didn't know, but thought it had something to do with feeling bad when you "kicked girls or little dogs." And a nine-year-old explained it as a voice inside that says no when you want to do something like beat up your little brothers.[1] One junior higher I know answered the same question by saying that a guilty conscience was "that sick feeling in the pit of your stomach when you realize you've just blown it."

Guilt, however, can be positive. Can you imagine what this world would be like if people didn't have consciences and didn't feel guilty when they did wrong? If human beings felt no guilt, the world probably wouldn't make it through another day. It would explode with sin.

Thousands and thousands of people are in psychiatric hospitals today because, for one reason or another, they aren't able to deal with their feelings of guilt. I wish these people could understand that although guilty feelings have a necessary role in our lives, the great news of the gospel of Jesus Christ is that we can be *forgiven*. The guilt that drives us to seek forgiveness is then washed away.

I believe many people do not become Christians because they can't believe that the good news—the gospel—of Jesus Christ is true. They keep waiting for the catch to the story. But there is no catch. In Jesus Christ we can find forgiveness for our sins—past, present, and future! His death on the cross was the penalty He paid for your sins; the resurrection from the tomb was His victory over sin and death and the gift of life for you. I know that idea is hard to understand, but nevertheless, it is the truth. Consider the following story.

Nicole's Story

Nicole grew up in a basic middle-class American home. Her family seemed to fight more than the average family, but otherwise it was pretty much normal. They were not necessarily Christians, but in seventh grade Nicole went to church camp and decided to give her life to Jesus Christ. She became active in her church youth group, but peer pressure began to get to her and she experimented with light drugs and sex. One night when she was a tenth grader, she got a little high and her twelfth-grade boyfriend convinced her to go all the way. It was against her Christian principles, but she did it anyway. From that time on, she seemed to slip downhill emotionally. Life went on, but this one negative experience paralyzed her faith, her belief in herself, and her emotions.

I talked with her when she was in her early twenties. She still seemed paralyzed by guilt. After listening to her story, I asked her if she had ever asked Jesus Christ to forgive her for this past sin that kept haunting her. Nicole replied, "Yes, almost every day since it happened in tenth grade." Eight years later, she was still pleading for God's forgiveness.

I then asked her what I thought was a simple question: "Do you believe God has forgiven you?"

Her answer gave me insight into her problem. She replied, "I really don't see how He could ever forgive me."

Although Nicole was a Christian, she didn't understand the core of the gospel of Jesus Christ. We all do some pretty rotten things in life, but there is absolutely nothing that God will not forgive. God forgave our sins now and forever because of the sacrifice of Jesus on the cross.

Nicole needed to know—*really* know and believe in her innermost heart—that the very first time she asked for God's forgiveness, He had completely forgiven her. Her problem was that she would not accept His forgiveness and she wouldn't forgive herself. Therefore, she carried around a load of *false* guilt that was ruining her life. Nicole was living with the emotional and physical consequences of poor decisions. But because of the love and grace of God, she could experience a "secondary virginity." Spiritually speaking, secondary virginity is when God totally forgives you for your sin and looks at you as a brand-new person.

As you can see, God's ways are different from our ways. Humans tend to hold grudges and break off relationships. God, however, always forgives. He always works to give His children new lives. If you have not yet asked Jesus Christ to become part of your life, these next two paragraphs are for you.

Invite Christ Into Your Life

The ultimate act of love was Jesus' death on the cross for you. The Bible says, "God demonstrates his own love for us in this: While we were still sinners, Christ died for us" (Romans 5:8). I believe the most important decision in life is to acknowledge Christ's work on the cross and to invite Him to live within you. When you invite Christ to live in your life, He does a number of things immediately. I'll mention just a few: He forgives your sins; He dwells within you; He gives you eternal life; and He offers you an abundant life on earth.

If you have never asked Jesus Christ to come into your life, I urge you to do so right now. If you say the following simple prayer to God sincerely, your life will be transformed from the inside out. If you do say this prayer to God, then I urge you to get involved with Christians who will help you understand your new faith and will help you to grow as a new, forgiven believer. Here's the prayer:

> *Almighty God, I love you. Thank you for the supreme sacrifice of love in Jesus Christ's death on the cross. I ask Jesus to come into my life and to forgive my sins. Thank you for setting me free. Amen.*

Eventually, Nicole did work through her guilt feelings and accepted the freedom and forgiveness Jesus offers. Today she is a happy, vibrant woman who understands that the forgiveness of Jesus Christ is a *free* gift given to all who ask. The Bible says, "If we confess our sins, he is faithful and just and will forgive us our sins and purify us from all unrighteousness" (1 John 1:9).

Perhaps you are a believer who has a story similar to Nicole's. Now is the time to get rid of your guilt by asking Jesus Christ to forgive your sins. He is faithful to forgive you 100 percent of the time. When you ask, He forgives you, and you never have to feel guilty again.

One time someone asked me, "Aren't you afraid that people will sin more if you tell them about God's complete forgiveness?"

I replied, "Of course not! When a person really understands the unconditional love and forgiveness of Jesus Christ, the desire for obedience will be greater than the desire to sin." And I pray that you will believe this good news of Jesus Christ so that you will no longer be paralyzed by your guilt. The gift of forgiveness is yours for the asking. How can you pass up such an offer of love and total acceptance?

Things to Think About

1. Why is it so difficult to overcome our guilt feelings?
2. Think of Nicole's inability to completely believe that God

forgave her. What are some specific differences between real guilt and false guilt?

3. What makes it difficult for you to accept God's forgiveness?

4. What would you tell someone who has a guilty conscience?

Respect Builders

1. All human beings have experienced—and many continue to experience—guilt for a variety of sins in their lives. In His great love, God provides a way for us to leave behind our guilt. He promises us forgiveness for our sins. There is no limit to this forgiveness. We need only to confess our failings to Him, and He gladly forgives us.

   Take a moment to write on a piece of paper every sin that comes to your mind. Ask God to forgive you of your sin and cleanse your life. Remember, His forgiveness is for the asking. Then either tear up, burn, or throw away the paper as a sign of God's complete forgiveness.

2. Here are some questions that will help you deal with forgiving others:

   • When have you struggled to forgive someone? Be specific about the circumstances.

   • Why was it hard for you to forgive that person? What were you feeling?

   • When have you asked for forgiveness for something you said or did? Describe the situation.

   • How did you feel about approaching the person you had hurt or disappointed?

• What is the greatest act of forgiveness by any ordinary human being that you know about personally?

Team Effort

A Bible study on forgiveness:

The story of David and Bathsheba in 2 Samuel 11–12 illustrates how even great men of God make mistakes. Read the story as a group, and then let each person share what he or she thinks caused David to do the things he did.

To conclude this discussion, read through Psalm 51. Ask the group how the emotions of guilt and pain David experienced relate to their lives.

What do these verses say about God?
Psalm 86:5

Psalm 103:3

What did God do that we might be forgiven and live in a right relationship with Him?
John 3:16

Romans 5:8

What does God do with our confessed sin?
1 John 1:9

Once a sin is confessed and forgiven, does God remember it? Look up the following verses. Write them down to impress upon your mind what God does with confessed, forgiven sin.
Psalm 103:12

Isaiah 43:25

Micah 7:19

If God forgets your sins and buries them in the sea, there is never any reason for you to go fishing for them!

Chapter Sixteen

Options for the Pregnant

One of the reasons I've written this book is so that the subject of this chapter will never become a reality in your life. Unfortunately, in the United States alone, more than one million unwed girls and women become pregnant each year.[1] Far too many times (perhaps most of the time), the people involved have not thought through the options until it is too late. Furthermore, oftentimes the pregnant girl is left to make some difficult decisions on her own because her partner has conveniently removed himself from the scene and is nowhere to be found.

To be honest, all the options for an unwed mother-to-be are lousy. All the options are complicated. All the options will cause a great deal of hurt and pain. Sometimes the difficulties are so great that the girls simply won't admit they are pregnant. They repress every thought about the subject until they actually believe they are not pregnant—even after "the signs" begin to show. Too many girls do not make decisions about their pregnancies because they simply wish it to go away. But it won't.

What can you do if you are pregnant or you get a girl pregnant? Here are some steps to take.

Helpful Steps for Pregnant Girls

First of all, take a pregnancy test. Be 100 percent sure you are pregnant. If you have had sexual intercourse and have missed your period or if you are even a little late, get checked as soon as possible. There is no sense in second-guessing your body. The sooner you know for sure, the more time you will have to think through your options.

Today there are many easy ways to find out if you are pregnant. It takes approximately ten days after intercourse to know for sure, and methods are being researched as of this writing that could possibly reveal a pregnancy within ten days of conception.[2] Early Pregnancy Tests (EPTs) are available without a prescription at local drugstores, or you can go to your doctor, a hospital outpatient clinic, or a free clinic in your local area. If you use the Early Pregnancy Test and it indicates you are pregnant, then you should immediately go to your doctor for confirmation and for instruction in prenatal care.

If you find out you are pregnant, don't face it alone. Share your situation with a person you trust. The best option is to sit down with one or both of your parents and have an open and honest conversation. Nine times out of ten, you'll find that you will receive more support than you expected. If you can't talk with your parents, find someone—a youth worker at church, a counselor at school, or a trusted adult friend—in whom to confide. You need all the positive support you can get.

Then take a serious look at the options as rationally as possible.

During stressful times, people often make emotional decisions that are simply wrong choices. They mean well but fail to carefully consider all the options because of the emotional tension in their lives.

Melissa's Lament

At the age of twenty-five, Melissa told me her own story of sadness and grief. When she was eighteen she was the homecoming queen, a cheerleader, and a leader in her church's youth group. She became pregnant by an older guy who immediately told her she must get an abortion. Melissa felt confused, scared, and empty. Without telling family or friends, she went to another county in her state and had an abortion. It has been seven years and Melissa has still not told her friends or family. Of course, her "boyfriend" is long gone. She told me she really regretted having an abortion. She called it a "form of murder." Melissa cried, "I don't think I will ever be able to forgive myself." She had never dreamed she would be unmarried and pregnant. When she found herself in that predicament, she felt forced into aborting her baby. Now she lives to regret her actions.

I've heard too many similar stories. It always seems as though it is the good, well-meaning people who make mistakes by never dealing with all the options.

Choosing an Option Intelligently

My wife and I sat with Amber and Chris. They were both nineteen years old, intelligent, athletic, attractive, and not married. Amber was very (eight and a half months) pregnant. They were dealing with the difficult process of deciding whether to keep their baby or place the baby up for adoption. Neither choice was easy, and either one would change their lives forever. Their social worker, my wife, and I, however, sensed that although they were confused, eventually Amber and Chris would make the decision that would be right for them. They were thinking rationally and looking at the options despite the intense emotional nature of the situation.

Ultimately, Amber and Chris did place the baby up for adoption, and two very special Christian parents are making a wonderful home for this baby. I appreciated the maturity Chris and Amber displayed as they took the time to work through the decision confronting them.

Let's take a closer look at the possibilities. The three possible options are abortion, adoption, and keeping the child. All three have unique problems, but all three are options you must consider. This chapter will deal with two of the alternatives, and the next chapter will deal with abortion.

Options to Consider

Adoption

Although adoption is not as popular as it used to be, it is definitely still an important option. Adoption can be a positive alternative to abortion or keeping the baby. It can be a positive experience for the birth parents, the child, and the adoptive parents.

At seventeen, Shannon thought she was too young to raise the child she was carrying. Her boyfriend was being supportive to her through the pregnancy, but he wasn't ready to settle down. Seeking the help of a counselor, Shannon carefully considered the options and decided on adoption. The adoptive parents were in their late twenties and had been married for five years. They had been told they would never be able to have children of their own. They desperately wanted to raise children and give them a home. Arrangements for the adoption were made. Shannon was reassured that her child would be given to very special people who would provide a warm, loving home for the baby. When she delivered the baby, Shannon allowed the adoptive parents to take the child home from the hospital. Later, Shannon wrote a letter to the new parents. This is what she wrote:

Dear Parents of the Little Baby:

I want you to know that I pray for your—I mean "our"—child daily. As I look back on the decision to release my baby for adoption, it was the most difficult decision I have ever made.

But I want you to know that it was also the wisest decision I have ever made, and I know it's the best decision for the baby. I hope you'll tell the baby when he grows up that I love him and will always love him. Help him understand that I released him because I wanted the best for him.

Even though I've never met you and probably never will, I'm grateful to God for the love you have for "our" child.

With all my love,
Unsigned

Should you decide on adoption, make sure you select a respectable agency whose number-one desire is to give your baby the finest home possible. Make sure the agency, lawyer, or whoever handles the adoption does a thorough home study of the adoptive family. Some birth parents choose the adoptive family and others have the agency choose. One of the biggest issues in the mind of every birth parent is whether the baby will live in a happy, secure home that is filled with love and support. When a person is confident that the baby will be in such a home, it is easier to release the baby to adoptive parents.

Keeping the Baby

An option that more and more young people are choosing is to raise the baby themselves (and often with a lot of help from their parents). Here I have mixed emotions. Of course, if a young person can handle the responsibility of raising a child, she should strongly consider keeping the baby. Most young people, however, have a terribly difficult time managing their own problems, let alone constant pleas for love and attention from someone else. I'm saddened by the amount of child abuse that consequently occurs among teenage parents. The statistics are frightening.

If you are pregnant and trying to make a decision about keeping the baby, ask yourself these questions: What is the best for the baby? Will I get married to the father? Am I emotionally stable enough to handle the constant demands of being a parent? Also, make sure you get help from a counselor. I know several great kids who were born to teenage parents who have turned out fine. I also know some young people who have been raised by teenage parents and have had real emotional struggles because of being raised in a difficult home situation. Your decision to keep the child must be a personal decision, but get the advice and help of people who sincerely love you and want the best for you and the baby.

Charlie Shedd wrote a great book on sex entitled *The Stork Is Dead*. Written years ago, it still offers what seems to be timeless insight. He quotes, for instance, a letter written to him by a young girl on what it's like to be married at age seventeen. It's worth reprinting here.

Jimmy and I couldn't wait so now we are married. Big deal!

Let me tell you what it is like to be married at 17. It is like living in this dump on the third floor up and your only window looks out on somebody else's third floor dump.

It is like coming home at night so tired you feel like you're dead from standing all day at your waitressing job. But you don't dare sit down because you might never get up again and there are so many things to do like cooking and washing and dusting and ironing. So you go through the motions and you hate your job and you ask yourself, "Why don't I quit?" and you already know why. It's because there are grocery bills and drug bills and rent bills and doctor bills, and Jimmy's crummy little check from the lumberyard won't cover them, that's why!

Then you try to play with the baby until Jimmy comes home. Only sometimes you don't feel like playing with her. But even if you do, you get this awful feeling that you are only doing it because you feel guilty. She is so beautiful, and you know it isn't fair for her to be in that old lady's nursery all day long. Then you change diapers and mix formula and you hate it, and you wonder how long it will be till she can tell how you feel, and wouldn't it be awful if she could tell already?

Then Jimmy doesn't come home, and you know it's because he is out with the boys doing the things he didn't get to do because you had to get married. So, finally you go to bed and cry yourself to sleep telling yourself that it really is better when he doesn't come home because sometimes he says the cruelest things. Then you ask yourself "Why does he hate me so much?" And you know it is because he feels trapped, and he doesn't love you anymore, like he said he would.

Then he comes home and he wakes you up, and he starts saying all the nice things he said before you got married. But you know it is only because he wants something, and yet you want to believe that maybe it is the old Jimmy again. So you give in, but when he gets what he wants, he turns away and you know he was only using you once more. So you try to sleep but you can't. This time, you cry silently because you don't want to admit that you care.

You lie there and think. You think about your parents and your brothers and the way they teased you. You think about your backyard and the swing and the tree house and all the things you had when you were little. You think about the good meals your mother cooked and how she tried to talk to you, but you were so sure she had forgotten what it was like to be in love.

Then you think about your girlfriends and the fun they must be having at the prom. You think about the college you planned to go to, and you wonder who will get the scholarship they promised you. You wonder who you would have dated in college and who you might have married and what kind of a job would he have had?

Suddenly you want to talk, so you reach over and touch Jimmy. But he is far away and he pushes you aside, so now you can cry yourself to sleep for real.

If you ever meet any girls like me who think they are just too smart to listen to anyone, I hope you'll tell them that this is what it is like to be married at seventeen.[3]

As this story, and the entire chapter, has pointed out, the decision facing unwed teenage mothers and fathers is not an easy one. If you find yourself in this situation, it is important that you think through the options as carefully and as unemotionally as possible. It is also important that you really try to listen to the advice of those people who care about you and whom you can trust. The Bible is clear when it says, "Where there is no guidance, a people falls; but in an abundance of counselors there is safety" (Proverbs 11:14 RSV). Also, lean on God for His strength in this difficult time, for His answers to your prayers for guidance and for the peace He offers to His children.

Things to Think About

1. Why do you think some girls deny they are pregnant?
2. Who do you know who would be helpful to talk to about subjects such as this? Consider, for example, your parents, youth worker, minister, a school counselor, or an adult friend.
3. What advice would you give a girl who is pregnant?
4. Read Psalm 139:13–17. How do these verses relate to a couple who is making a decision about a pregnancy?

Respect Builders

1. Read Psalm 139. Jot down some sentences and phrases that speak of God's love and concern for you.

2. Visit a Christian crisis pregnancy center with a friend, your youth group, or a family member and ask for a presentation on options for people who are pregnant. You may even want to invite them to make a presentation at your church or school.

Team Effort

To consider the pros and cons of adoption and keeping the baby, complete the following chart. List arguments for and against each choice from the viewpoint of the baby's mother, the baby's father, the baby's grandparents (that is, the parents of the baby's father and mother), and the baby himself/herself. Discuss these with your group.

	Adoption	Keeping the Baby
Baby's Mother *Pros*		
Cons		
Baby's Father *Pros*		
Cons		
Baby's Grandparents *Pros*		
Cons		
Baby *Pros*		
Cons		

Chapter Seventeen

What About Abortion?

Seldom in our nation's history has there been a more emotional issue than that of abortion. I realize you may be receiving some confusing and contradictory information. In our fallen world, whether we like it or not, abortion has become an option. *However*, let me say it as clearly as I can: In my opinion, abortion is *not* an option. My heart bleeds for young women who get pregnant outside of marriage, and I feel deeply for women who have already chosen to abort their babies. I know it's a complicated decision. Yet the fact remains that regardless of the circumstances of pregnancy, the baby developing inside the womb is a person who deserves as much attention and protection as his or her mother.

Some people will tell you the baby is only a fetus and not a person. Yet on day one of the pregnancy, the "sperm joins with the ovum (egg) to form one cell. This new life has inherited 23 chromosomes from each parent, 46 in all. This one cell contains the complex genetic blueprint for every detail of human development—the child's sex, hair and eye color, height and skin tone."[1]

That's all on the first day! At three weeks old, the heart is already beating. Brain waves can be detected and recorded at forty days. At just over twelve weeks, the baby sleeps, awakens, and can actually exercise its muscles. Fine hair has already begun to grow on the baby's head.

Cathy and I began to feel our daughter's movements by eighteen weeks. Many people still get abortions at eighteen weeks! I personally know women who have had abortions. They have confided to me that they can't forget the abortion no matter how hard they try. The term for this is "post abortion syndrome." Often a woman who has had an abortion will suffer deep grief about the loss of her baby. She will struggle with intense fear, anger, sadness, and guilt, knowing she has allowed a living baby in her womb to be killed.

Choosing Life

Stephanie was one of the leaders in our youth group. She wanted to become either a youth worker in the church or an attorney. Stephanie got great grades. She was loved by her peers and was one of my favorite people. When she came into my office and told me she was pregnant, I was shocked. She had experimented with sexual intercourse one time, got pregnant, and now had come to tell me she was going to get an abortion.

Stephanie said, "I know how you feel about abortion, Jim, but I wanted to tell someone before I did it. My parents [who were leaders in our church] would be embarrassed. I want to go on to college, and if I have a baby my life would be ruined forever." What would you have said to Stephanie if you were me?

First, I assured her I loved her. I thanked her for sharing her problem with me. She did most of the talking, and it was important for me to listen. After all, listening is the language of love. Finally, when she had said what was on her mind, she asked for my opinion.

That afternoon in my office we discussed all the issues. How would she feel about herself after an abortion, knowing in her heart that she had had a living human being inside her? We talked about sharing the news of her pregnancy with her parents. Sure they would be disappointed, but not half as disappointed as if they knew she was getting an abortion without talking to them about it first. We discussed the other options of keeping the baby or placing the baby in a wonderful home through adoption. I shared with her Cathy's and my struggle with infertility and the strong desire to adopt a child. We talked on and on.

Stephanie admitted that in the strong emotional turmoil of her life, she had not taken some of these factors into consideration. It was important for her to look at all sides of the issue. Because Stephanie was a Christian, it was important to look at the Bible. Together, Stephanie and I read:

> *So God created man in his own image, in the image of God he created him; male and female he created them.* (Genesis 1:27)

> *Sons (and daughters!) are a heritage from the Lord, children a reward from him.* (Psalm 127:3, parentheses mine)

> *For you created my inmost being; you knit me together in my mother's womb. I praise you because I am fearfully and wonderfully made; your works are wonderful, I know that full well. My frame was not hidden from you when I was made in the secret place. When I was woven together in the depths of the earth, your eyes saw my unformed*

body. All the days ordained for me were written in your book before one of them came to be. (Psalm 139:13–16)

Listen to me, you islands; hear this, you distant nations: Before I was born the Lord called me; from my birth he has made mention of my name. (Isaiah 49:1)

For by him all things were created: things in heaven and on earth, visible and invisible, whether thrones or powers or rulers or authorities; all things were created by him and for him. (Colossians 1:16)

After looking at the Scripture references, Stephanie and I prayed and cried. I asked her if she was willing to give this baby inside her over to God. She nodded. That evening, together, we talked with her parents. They were shocked, yes, but more understanding than Stephanie imagined.

Stephanie made an appointment with an excellent Christian crisis pregnancy center. After much counsel, many difficult decisions, and an incredible amount of support, she chose to release her baby for adoption. Today, years later, Stephanie is helping other unwed mothers. She is happily married and a deeply committed Christian. Today, somewhere in a Christian home, a little boy has two parents who love him and are raising their "Matthew," which means gift from God. Thank God for Stephanie. Thank God she had the courage to make the right decision and not necessarily the easy decision.

One last thought. I have this feeling if Jesus Christ were here He would say, "I died to redeem the lost, the crippled, the sinners, the innocent, and defenseless babies who are in the wombs of mothers." I think He would stand loud and clear on the side of protecting innocent unborn babies, because they too have the incredible potential of someday becoming instruments of the kingdom of God.

Please don't sit on the fence on this issue. Make a decision that abortion is not an option for you. Choose life.

Things to Think About

1. What makes abortion the easy way out of the problem but not the right way?
2. What do you suppose God's view of abortion is?
3. Why do you think abortion is such a controversial subject?
4. Why was Stephanie's decision to give her baby to God and not get an abortion a difficult one? What were the positive consequences of her decision?

Respect Builders

1. Make a decision to choose life and stand on the side of innocent unborn children. You can do this by (a) never being involved in an abortion yourself; (b) working to make sure people hear the side of the unborn; and (c) praying and caring for the burdens of unwed mothers and fathers.

2. Acquire some excellent resources on abortion and become acquainted with the important issues around this significant subject.

Team Effort

Case Study: Values

Brittany was seventeen and had a lot going in her favor. She was an intelligent and beautiful girl. Schoolwork had always been easy for her. Her nearly straight-A average indicated that she was a perfect candidate for an Ivy League university. She dreamed of becoming a lawyer and a politician.

Brittany was respected by her peers and was sought after as a friend. She had dated several guys from her youth group and church during the past year and a half. Brittany began dating a young man she met at church who was in the military service. His name was Jeff. He was a nice person who had recently moved to her community from another state. He was lonely and loved the positive atmosphere of Brittany's circle of friends, church, and home.

A few months after her relationship with Jeff became serious, Brittany came to the office of her youth worker. It was easy to tell she had been crying for hours. Between sobs, she blurted out this story: "Jeff and I went 'all the way' once. That month I missed my period but I didn't think much about it. The next month I missed my period and went to a doctor. I am pregnant. I told Jeff. He gave me money for an abortion and told me he is transferring away from the area and never wants to see me again. I don't want to tell my family. And I don't want to carry a baby and be a disgrace to all I've stood for. If I keep the baby, I'll ruin my chances for going to law school."

Although Brittany had never been a supporter of abortion, she shared with her youth worker that she had made an appointment to get one in two days.

1. What factors in Brittany's situation added to her feeling of hurt?
2. Because Brittany had already made an appointment for an abortion, what might she have been seeking from her youth worker?

3. If you were the youth worker, what would you say? What would you do?

4. In what ways might Brittany's parents react? How might their reactions affect Brittany?

5. Read Psalm 139:13–16. How does this passage relate to this case study?

Chapter Eighteen

Masturbation

The word "masturbation" causes strange reactions in most people. Masturbation is, however, an experience most people have had, yet seldom does anyone talk about it. And when so-called experts discuss or write about the subject, they can't seem to agree on whether it is right or wrong.

Some people are uncertain about what masturbation actually is. Technically, masturbation is called "autoeroticism." *Auto* means *self* and *eroticism* means *sexual stimulation*. Put the words together and you have "self sexual stimulation." Masturbation is usually the first sexual behavior for both guys and girls. Often you'll find little children handling their genitals and exploring their bodies, but even then their parents may discourage this behavior.

Several years ago I was a counselor at a Christian camp. I was working with eight high-school guys. Somehow, in our morning Bible study time, the subject of masturbation came up. Before lunch, the word was out: "Jim is willing to talk about masturbation!" Before lunch was finished, the man in charge of the camp had pulled me aside to ask just what we were talking about during the Bible study hour. I told him the same thing I told the guys in my cabin and am telling you. Incidentally, before the camp had ended, at least twenty high schoolers asked if they could talk with me privately about their problem. This experience says to me that it is time we become more open about this important subject and help people deal with their "problem" in an intelligent manner.

A majority of people (especially guys) have had a masturbation experience by the time they turn eighteen. A person is not abnormal if he or she has never had the experience, and a person is not abnormal if he or she has had it. Studies tell us that in the last twenty-five years, many more girls have masturbated than ever before. I've read statistics that say between 50 and 80 percent of all girls have had a masturbation experience. I've heard it said that 92 percent of all males have had the experience and the other 8 percent are liars! In other words, almost all males have masturbated at least once. I tell you these statistics because far too many people believe they are among just a few people in the world who masturbate. They are completely wrong.

"Okay, Jim, but let's get to the point: Is masturbation wrong? Is it a sin?" I wish the Bible spoke to this issue more clearly. Jesus was very clear about the issue of lust, and I find it difficult to understand that a person could have a masturbation experience very often without lusting in his or her heart. In today's world, masturbation is often equated with viewing pornography online, and I am strongly opposed to any type of pornography viewing because of what it does to your mind and view of healthy sexuality. However, when it comes to the issue of masturbation, you must make up your own mind. You must intelligently work through the decision. And I would suggest that you turn to God for help. Let me give you two opposing viewpoints from two outstanding Christian people to help you arrive at your decision.

Opposing Views on Masturbation

When I was in high school I read two opposing views. Both of these views are prevalent today. In his book *This Is Loving?* David Wilkerson says, "Masturbation is not a gift of God for sex drives. Masturbation is not moral behavior and is not condoned in the Scriptures. . . . Masturbation is not harmless fun."[1] On the other hand, Dr. Charlie Shedd, a much respected Christian authority on sex and dating, does call masturbation a "gift of God." He claims that masturbation "can be a positive factor in your total development" and goes on to say that "teenage masturbation is preferable to teenage intercourse. It is better to come home hot and bothered than satisfied and worried."[2]

My own view is somewhere in between these two extremes. Masturbation is practically universal. It isn't the gross sin some think it is, yet at times it can have a negative side to it.

Negative Factors of Masturbation

Specifically, uncontrolled masturbation can be very negative. Psychologists call this kind of behavior "obsessive-compulsive." This means that a person can become so consumed with masturbation that it takes over his or her mind and actions. One young man confided to me that he figured he masturbated ten to fifteen times a week and that this one experience had completely taken over his mind. He had tremendous guilt feelings, was withdrawing more and more into himself, and was afraid to be with people. His obsessive-compulsive behavior was destroying his self-image, his relationship with God, and his relationships with other people. We had to help him work through his negative habit and change his behavior.

Another negative effect is uncontrolled fantasy. Jesus loves us unconditionally and yet He calls us to high standards. When discussing the question of lust, for instance, Jesus said, "You have heard that it was said, 'Do not commit adultery.' But I tell you that anyone who looks at a woman lustfully has already committed adultery with her in his heart. If your right eye causes you to sin, gouge it out and throw it away. It is better for you to lose one part of your body than for your whole body to be thrown into hell" (Matthew 5:27–29). When masturbation leads a guy or girl to have uncontrolled fantasies, God calls it sin.

Often people who struggle with an overactive fantasy life are viewing porn online, reading pornographic literature, watching X-rated movies, and constantly placing themselves in a position to be aroused by sexually stimulating material. I believe pornographic material will help lead anyone down the wrong path.

One more thing. If you are filled with negative guilt feelings and a real sense of insecurity, don't suffer in silence. Although it is a difficult subject to discuss, share your feelings and questions with someone you can trust. Your feelings might be well founded, but on the other hand, they might simply be false guilt.

The Not-So-Negative Factors

I'm afraid that too many times well-meaning parents, friends, teachers, and ministers have added coals to the fire when they tell kids, "If you do it, you will become sterile, blind, mentally ill, or homosexual." Those suggestions contain no truth whatsoever. Whatever else can be said about masturbation, most doctors, scientists, psychologists, and ministers now agree that it will not harm you biologically. Let me repeat an earlier statement: If you've had the experience, you are normal; if you haven't, you are also normal.

To be perfectly honest, as a Christian, I wish the Bible gave us a clear answer. It does not. The Bible simply does not discuss this issue. As much as I would like to give you "the answer," I cannot. There isn't one. This is a subject you will have to work through alone or with the help of someone you trust. The book of James gives some solid advice: "If any of you lacks wisdom, he should ask God, who gives generously to all without finding fault, and it will be given to him" (James 1:5). Let God help you make a decision that is glorifying to Him. Remember, He created you—and your sexual identity!

Things to Think About

1. Why do you think people are so silent about masturbation?
2. If someone has a problem with masturbation, who could that person go to for a serious, confidential conversation?
3. I mentioned the words "uncontrolled fantasy." How can that be a negative factor?
4. Do you believe I was right or wrong to discuss the topic of masturbation with the high-school guys at the camp? Do you think adults should talk openly with teenagers about sex and related matters?

Respect Builders

1. Based on this chapter and other input you may have received on this subject, develop your opinion on the subject of masturbation.

What are the arguments in favor of and against masturbation? In what context can masturbation be a problem?

2. Where do you stand on the issue? Because the Bible does not make a clear statement about masturbation, it may be possible that it is not a matter of crucial importance to God. Consider, for instance, the attention the Bible gives to idolatry, murder, premarital sex, and gossip! God does, however, want you to be a useful, growing Christian, and anything that keeps you from being such a person is to be avoided. So if masturbation is keeping you from growing in Him, you might need to do something about it. Make sure you decide for yourself what you should do. Base your decision on prayer and on what you know about the Lord and His will for your life.

Team Effort

In this chapter, two views are given about masturbation: Dr. Shedd's and David Wilkerson's. Of these two views, do you think either one of them is more in line with the general principles of Scripture than the other? Talk about the pros and cons of each view.

Chapter Nineteen

AIDS

Eric Nolan (not his real name) grew up in a small Texas town. He had two older brothers and great parents, and all of them were active in their local Southern Baptist church. As Eric grew older, he seriously considered going into the ministry. He had preached a few sermons and had been a leader in his youth group. No one knew that Eric struggled with his gender identity. Eric was confused about this part of his life. He had been involved with girlfriends in the past, but one night he had a homosexual experience. It wasn't something he had planned on having, but nevertheless, it happened. Eventually, Eric decided to take up the homosexual lifestyle. He suffered a large amount of guilt as he lived a life of constant partying, barhopping, and promiscuity. His life grew more and more unhappy. He eventually came back around and sought the faith of his childhood. Eric had the courage to leave his life of homosexual promiscuity and return to the Lord. He found a girlfriend, he went back to college, and he even chose to be re-baptized at the new church he was attending. Things were actually going great for Eric.

At first, when he started getting sick so often, he assumed it was a bad virus. Doctors couldn't determine what was wrong. Then came the pronouncement that must be on the mind of everyone who has ever engaged in homosexuality or had a sexually promiscuous, heterosexual lifestyle. Eric Nolan had contracted AIDS. It's true, Eric had come back to the Lord and changed his way of living, but the HIV virus had been dormant in his body since his homosexual days. Eric struggled with AIDS for several years. His strong Christian faith and the love of his family and friends kept him tough to the end, but AIDS kills, and Eric was no exception. His funeral was a mixture of joy because of his relationship with God and sorrow that Eric was another victim of this terrible disease.

The Basics of AIDS

AIDS is caused by a virus (HIV) that attacks and eventually destroys the human immune system. As you probably already know, the word *AIDS* is an acronym that combines the first letters of the four words that make up the disease's scientific name:

Acquired **I**mmune **D**eficiency **S**yndrome

Acquired means that a person gets the disease during his or her life. In the case of AIDS, most teenagers who acquire the disease do so by sexual involvement or when sharing needles during drug use.

Immune means that AIDS attacks the human immune system. Your immune system is what defends your body against diseases such as infections and cancers.

Deficiency means that AIDS destroys or generally weakens the immune system. When enough damage is done, a person no longer has the ability to fight off other diseases and dies.

Syndrome is a medical term that refers to a group of medical symptoms.

The HIV virus enters the body in two primary ways: through intimate sexual contact or through intravenous drug use. About 75 percent of AIDS cases come from intimate sexual contact, and approximately 20 percent of AIDS cases are related to using a needle to inject drugs directly into the body.

It used to be thought that most HIV carriers are homosexual; however, the statistics are changing—particularly in Africa, where unprotected heterosexual promiscuity has caused the virus to spread at alarming rates. Two things are necessary for a person infected with HIV to transmit the virus to a healthy person. First, the infected person must transfer a body fluid that contains the virus to the healthy person. HIV has been found in blood, sexual body fluids, and saliva. Second, the body fluid carrying the virus must *enter* the body of the healthy person. This can happen through a cut, a small scrape, or a mucous membrane. Basically, authorities tell us that intimate sexual contact with a partner who has HIV is, and will continue to be, the main way of "catching" the virus.

Although the percentages are low, HIV can also be transmitted in a few other ways. A mother who has HIV or AIDS in her blood can infect her unborn baby. Also, a small number of medical workers have been infected with HIV by "needle sticks." This happens when workers accidentally jab themselves with needles that contain the blood of an AIDS patient. Finally, blood transfusions with AIDS-infected blood account for approximately 3 percent of all AIDS cases.

The reason I take the time to explain some of the basics of AIDS is because many people do not have the straight facts. Either they underestimate the risk with an "it-will-never-happen-to-me" attitude, or they are running scared with the misconception that you can get AIDS from swimming pools or public toilets.

Be Informed About AIDS

Remember, the best way to avoid getting HIV and AIDS is to *avoid intimate sexual contact.*

Today, probably the greatest risk of getting HIV comes from having sex before marriage. Not everyone who has sex before marriage will get AIDS, but obviously, the more sexual contact and sexual partners a person has, the greater the chance of getting it. In some classrooms today, you will hear about "safe sex." To put it bluntly, there is no such thing. The fact is that "safe sex" practices often do not protect a person. These practices fail for many reasons. One, the person may not do everything exactly right at the right times when it comes to protection. Alcohol or drugs might affect judgment and cause a person to make mistakes. There may be failures beyond a person's control. No birth control device is 100 percent fail-safe in protecting a person from the AIDS virus.

Whenever you hear someone talk about "safe sex," think of the following example. If you were to take a revolver and put a bullet in one of its six chambers, then point the gun at your head and pull the trigger, it would be "safer" than if you had filled five of the six chambers with bullets. The risk is less, but you can hardly call it "safe." The safest thing to do is *don't do it at all.*

Before this chapter ends, we must deal again with the issue of drugs. One of the easiest ways to contract AIDS is to inject yourself with drugs by using a "dirty" needle. Drug users often share needles.

Someone else's blood may remain on the needle, and you may just inject that person's infected blood into your body.

The other problem with drugs—and alcohol too—is that your judgment is seriously affected. You may do some stupid things when you are drunk or high. One mistake is enough. With AIDS, once is all it takes.

Things to Think About

1. Why is it important to get the straight facts on AIDS?
2. If a person chooses sexual abstinence before marriage, how possible is it to get AIDS?
3. Why do you suppose a chapter on AIDS would include a message on drugs and drinking?
4. What can Christians do for people who have AIDS?

Respect Builders

1. If you have ever had sexual contact or used a needle for drugs, get a test for HIV immediately. The earlier the AIDS virus is found, the more that can be done. Some people have died an earlier death because of the embarrassment of getting tested for AIDS. If you have had sexual contact or used a needle for drugs, you can get tested anonymously. You do not need parental consent to get the test.

2. Volunteer to help HIV and AIDS victims. Obviously, people suffering from AIDS are in need. This is a time to show them the love of God. Many excellent organizations need volunteers to read, visit, run errands, and share resources with AIDS victims.

Check with your pastor or youth worker to find out what you can do in your community.

Team Effort

AIDS: A curse or natural consequence?

Divide into two groups and debate the issue of AIDS by discussing the following statements:

1. AIDS is a curse from God, *or* AIDS is a natural consequence of our fallen world.
2. AIDS victims should not be allowed to live in public, *or* AIDS victims should receive all the freedoms of anyone else.
3. A doctor who has AIDS should quit his or her medical practice immediately, *or* a doctor who has AIDS has the same rights as any other doctor.
4. A teacher who has AIDS should quit teaching students, *or* a teacher who has AIDS may continue to teach as long as he or she is healthy.
5. Homosexuality is a worse sin than adultery or fornication, *or* homosexuality is no different from adultery or fornication.

Chapter Twenty

Sexually Transmitted Diseases (STDs)

When it comes to the subject of venereal disease, most of us try to forget that it exists. *Venereal* refers to something related to or transmitted by sexual activity. *Venereal disease* is any one of several diseases contracted mainly through sexual activity; such illnesses are also called *STDs* or sexually transmitted diseases. Each year, more than nineteen million cases of venereal disease are reported in the United States. Chlamydia now ranks second only to the common cold among communicable diseases. And, because more people are having casual sex these days, the spread of STDs is at an epidemic level, according to the American Medical Association. I believe, therefore, that it is important for every person, sexually active or not, to understand venereal disease, the symptoms, the consequences, and the treatments. In no way is this chapter or the previous chapter about AIDS meant to be a thorough examination of sexually transmitted diseases, but we all must become more aware of this growing epidemic among young people.

Chlamydia

Chlamydia is by far the most commonly reported infectious disease in the United States—nearly four million cases are reported *each year*! This bacterial infection is spread through sexual contact, and while it can be cured with antibiotics, its lack of obvious symptoms causes hundreds of thousands of people to suffer from the disease without even knowing it. The sad truth is that a large majority of those who contract chlamydia are women between the ages of fifteen and twenty-four, and the damage it can do to their reproductive systems is far worse than the effect the illness has on men. Undiagnosed and untreated, chlamydia can result in pelvic inflammatory disease, ectopic pregnancy (when the baby's placenta attaches in the Fallopian tubes rather than the uterus), and infertility. Studies have recently shown that many young women who have been treated for chlamydia are re-infected by the same male partner who unknowingly carries the disease.

Gonorrhea

Gonorrhea is the second most common of venereal diseases. Basically the only way to get the disease is through sexual contact. One dangerous feature of gonorrhea has earned it the name the "silent disease." Sometimes a person who has contracted it shows no major symptoms. A person may go for years without knowing he or she has the disease. In the meantime, serious physical damage may occur.

Usually, however, there are symptoms. Two to seven days after contact with someone who has gonorrhea, a woman might have a vaginal discharge, maybe mild pain upon urination and perhaps an abnormal menstrual period. A man's symptoms usually include a painful, burning sensation when he urinates and an uncomfortable discharge from the penis.

There is a cure for gonorrhea. Penicillin can cure the disease if it is found in the first stages. Without treatment, however, a person can become sterile (unable to produce children) because of damage to the sperm ducts or the Fallopian tubes. Gonorrhea has also been known to cause arthritis, meningitis, and heart disease. Another sad effect of gonorrhea is that it can cause blindness in an innocent baby at birth. These are not scare tactics about venereal disease—these are medical facts!

Genital Herpes

One of the most talked about forms of venereal disease is herpes simplex 2. Perhaps you have read about the outbreak of herpes in our country. Genital herpes is causing some sexually active people to at least be more selective about their partners, because at this time, there is no known cure for herpes.

Within three weeks of sexual contact with a partner infected by herpes, a person will develop blisters around the genitals. They may experience painful urination, fatigue, and swelling in the groin areas. The blisters will burst after a few days, leaving a discharge; then the symptoms will go away. This does not mean the symptoms will not come back. Periodically, the blisters and some of the other signs will appear, often without pain. The medical profession is desperately trying to find a cure, but so far all they have is treatment that may reduce pain and help prevent secondary infection.

Syphilis

Syphilis is a dangerous disease. Among communicable diseases, it is a major killer. If not treated in the first or second stages, syphilis can cause infections that will affect the heart, the brain, and the spinal cord, causing serious deterioration of the body. It is also considered a facilitator of HIV/AIDS because it increases the likelihood of spreading the disease.

Syphilis basically consists of three stages. The first symptom usually appears between ten and ninety days after contact. Usually a painless canker sore will appear on the penis or in or near the vagina. The canker sore will disappear after a few weeks. The second stage, which usually occurs between two and six months after contact, manifests itself as a rash all over the body and possibly a few sores on the sex organs. Tragically, by the time the disease reaches the third stage (often fifteen to twenty-five years after it has been contracted), it is difficult to treat. It can invade the nervous system, cause paralysis, and result in insanity. Blindness, swollen joints, and crippling can also come in the advanced stages of syphilis.

As you can see, and contrary to what you may have heard, venereal diseases are serious business. If you have even the slightest symptoms of a venereal disease, go immediately to a physician. Yes, it is embarrassing, but these diseases cannot be "wished" away. In the United States, for every reported case of venereal disease, there are thought to be two or three unreported cases. Perhaps some of those people do not recognize the signs, but many of them are simply afraid to report their symptoms. They wish and hope the signs will go away, and thus they risk suffering major physical consequences.

In our society, it is easy to be sexually promiscuous. Some people are in such desperate need of attention that they will go from one sex partner to another. Considering that venereal diseases are at epidemic levels, these people are playing with fire that literally can be deadly.

A young married man named Jim (no relationship, of course) talked with a nurse named Arvis Olsen and asked for the latest information on cures for herpes 2. Mrs. Olsen recorded this conversation in her excellent book *Sexuality: Guidelines for Teenagers*. Read Jim's comments carefully and look at the negative consequences he and his wife suffered.

Jim came to me and asked for the latest information on cures for herpes 2. "I got this pesky disease during college and have never been able to get rid of it. Every few months I get blisters, and then they disappear, only to return again later. I wasn't too worried about it until my wife's last visit to her doctor for her yearly checkup. He says she has to have a repeat on her Pap smear because the first test showed cell changes on her cervix. He told her that cervical cancers could be caused by the herpes virus, and he also told her she would be wise not to have any more children. We have only one child, Nurse, and I'm scared to death—let me add that all this has not done a lot for our marriage. If only I had known the consequences of the "fooling around" I did when I was nineteen! Marge and I could have the happiest marriage in the world, except . . . Those moments of pleasure were foolish, and the payment is unrelenting."[1]

Most people do not want to think about venereal diseases, and they especially do not want to think that it could happen to them. Yet statistics tell us that STDs continue to exist on an epidemic level. They won't go away just because people wish them to. Furthermore, sexually active young people need to know the facts about venereal diseases because the odds are in favor of a sexually active young person contracting one. One young friend of mine who contracted gonorrhea said to me, "It never entered my mind that I would get the disease. I thought it only happened to bad people. I don't think the sexual contact was worth the pain or humiliation."

Things to Think About

1. Do you think students are informed enough about venereal diseases?
2. Do kids at school ever talk about STDs?
3. What is your opinion of "casual sex"?
4. Do you think that because there is no cure for genital herpes some people will refrain from casual sex?

Respect Builders

1. Venereal diseases are generally brought on from casual sexual contact. Make a commitment today to *never* have casual sex. Casual sex is against God's standards, and considering the increase in venereal diseases and AIDS, it is far too dangerous to experience a moment of pleasure and a lifetime of sorrow.

2. List several reasons to refrain from sexual contact before marriage.

Team Effort

Venereal Disease: An unfortunate but natural part of a fallen world, or God's curse?

For discussion:

Some people think venereal disease is an unfortunate but natural part of our fallen world. Others think it is a punishment given by God to those who dare to be sexually promiscuous. They point to the occasional upsurge of a "new" form of venereal disease as an indication of the validity of their argument. How do you feel about this issue? List reasons for and against each view.

Natural Part of a Fallen World (reasons for and against)	God's Curse (reasons for and against)

Chapter Twenty-One

Homosexuality

When Adam came into our youth group several years ago, the group loved and accepted him immediately. It was easy to like him: He was fun loving, outgoing, athletic, and intelligent, and he had a real desire to grow in his newfound Christian faith. I wonder how the kids would have accepted him if they had known, as I did, that he was struggling with gender confusion. He wasn't sure if he was gay or straight. I would cringe when some of the other students in the group would tell "gay" jokes, or when guys would pretend to act feminine by holding a limp wrist in the air to get laughs. I would often catch myself stealing a quick glance at Adam. He never let on around the guys that it bothered him, but he sure let me know.

Adam and I would talk and talk about his feelings about possibly being gay and being Christian—which poses a good question: Can a person be a homosexual and a Christian at the same time? I believe all sexual immorality is sin. Heterosexuals who are having sex and not married are just as sinful as is a homosexual. Although the Bible calls the homosexual act a sin, in the same passage it lists envy, deceit, and gossip as being just as sinful as the homosexual act (see Romans 1:26–32).

Any discussion of homosexuality is complicated, but let's begin with the fact that all homosexuals are loved by God. He might not be pleased with the *act* of homosexuality, but He definitely loves the homosexual. All Christians should love homosexuals unconditionally, not for what they do or don't do, but for who they are. They are loved by our Lord just as much as heterosexuals are.

Who Is the Homosexual?

Many young people are confused about this subject, and one reason is that they may have had one homosexual experience and they think they might be gay. Many, perhaps most, young people do have what one might call a homosexual experience. Children, for instance, are curious and "play doctor" or engage in other kinds of experimentation. If this has happened to you, it does not mean you are a homosexual. It means that you, like millions of others before you, have had a normal childhood experience. Even if you as a teenager have had a few "homosexual experiences," this does not mean you are gay. A homosexual person is someone who has had continued sexual activity with others of the same sex and/ or is primarily attracted to those of the same sex. The person attracted to both sexes is called a bisexual. A new phrase that has become prevalent is "bi-curious," used to describe people who consider themselves heterosexual but have had homosexual thoughts or experiences on occasion. Because of the incredible amount of media attention, as well as a much more liberal culture, about 10 percent of the student population has struggled with gender identity confusion. This doesn't mean they are homosexual; it does mean that they are struggling with lots of confusion about their sexuality. We need to make sure that we don't write off everyone who thinks they *might* be gay as gay.

What Causes Homosexuality?

The cause of homosexuality remains a highly debated subject. Some experts believe homosexuality is genetic in origin. Others suggest that it comes from a hormonal imbalance. Some researchers believe very strongly that homosexuality is caused by a negative home environment, perhaps an overly dominant mother or a poor role model for a father. The best answer is that no one really knows exactly what causes homosexuality, and I'm sure the answer is probably a combination of some or all of the factors I've mentioned.

One thing is clear: If you struggle with homosexual or bisexual thoughts, you are not alone. One other thing is very clear. The Bible calls all sexual sin, sin, and yet God loves sinners. He does not reject one sin over another sin. I love what the excellent writer Tim Stafford wrote years ago when he was an editor for *Campus Life* magazine and wrote a monthly column to students about love, sex, and dating: "[Even if you believe] the condition has been given to you, you're accountable for how you respond."[1]

Many homosexuals blame other forces for their behavior. I understand their logic and I hurt for them, but I agree with Stafford. The homosexual has the final responsibility for his or her sexual behavior. I have met people who will probably have homosexual tendencies all their lives. They may be like alcoholics—once an alcoholic, always an alcoholic, even if they never indulge. Many Christians who do have a tendency toward homosexuality have, however, chosen to refrain from homosexual actions. The sin is in the actions, not the "tendency."

Most heterosexuals do not understand what it is like to struggle with gender identity issues. They view with repugnance the actions of practicing homosexuals. As Christians, however, we must take the biblical stance of unconditional love for homosexuals. I also believe that it is important for us to understand this problem, because within our culture, we will increasingly come into contact with people who are confused about their sexuality.

Homosexuals Need Counsel

If you think you might be homosexual, seek counsel. The longer you wait, the harder it will be to understand your sexual identity. Meet with a counselor you trust, and share with him or her your inner thoughts. You are not a freak! Many people share your confusion. Another piece of advice: When you are confused and hurting, don't drink or take drugs. Many sexually confused people resort to alcohol, pills, or marijuana to "overcome the problem." This "solution" doesn't work; it usually causes more problems.

Having encouraged you to seek counseling, I want to say one other important thing. If you want to change, I believe you can. First, it takes a strong desire to change. Second, you need God's supernatural power in your life to give you the extra support you need. Get involved in a church, read the Bible, and pray daily. Third, find a wise counselor who will listen to you, care about you, and hold you accountable to your resolution to change. It is also important to leave your friends who have had a negative influence on you and find a new set of friends who will be positive influences. Find friends who enjoy life and challenge you to be all that God desires you to be. I strongly recommend that you get involved with Christian friends and become active in a church.

A Story of Hope

Let me close this chapter by finishing the story of Adam, the guy from my youth group who struggled with the idea that he might be a homosexual. One day while on a youth group camping trip, he confided to me that he had been involved in various "gay" relationships for two years, yet he felt very unfulfilled and guilt ridden. He wanted to change but felt chained to his gay lifestyle. He asked if I could help.

Because Adam had a strong desire to change, I affirmed his desire and got him involved in some good counseling. For support, I went with him to his first appointment. Although the counseling was somewhat painful for Adam, it was also life changing. He moved to another area of our state but continued in counseling and became active in his new church. Today, Adam is married and has a child. He says, "God used the counseling, the strong support from Christian friends, and my church to free me from my bondage." With God's help and a loving community, people can change, and they do every day.

Things to Think About

1. Do you believe it is a sin to be homosexual? Why or why not?
2. What would you do if one of your friends confided in you that he or she is gay, lesbian, or bisexual?
3. Can you be a Christian and a homosexual?
4. Do you think it is okay to make fun of homosexuals? Why or why not?

Respect Builders

....

1. Make a decision today to never make fun of gay people. You may be repulsed by the idea of homosexual relationships, but you will never help a homosexual change with jokes, put-downs, or lack of love.

2. If you have a friend who is gay or lesbian, try to convince him or her to meet with a Christian counselor who can help deal with the issues. If you encourage someone to seek help and that person receives the help that is needed, then you have been used by God in a great way.

Team Effort

....

A Case Study: John

John is one of your best friends. He doesn't seem abnormal at all. He likes cars and sports, and he has been active in the church youth group with you. One night on a backpacking trip, you and John have a serious conversation. John tells you he thinks he is gay. He shares with you that he has had two homosexual experiences with an older neighbor and now he is really confused. He doesn't know if he is homosexual or heterosexual. He asks for your advice and friendship. As a group, talk about what you would say and do.

Chapter Twenty-Two

Pornography

Trevor is a popular, outgoing senior in his church and school. Trevor has more friends than anyone I know, and he has two great parents. *Trevor is addicted to pornography.*

It all started innocently enough when Trevor was younger. Trevor was spending the night with one of his best friends. His friend showed Trevor his favorite Internet porn sites as well as a stash of his father's old "girlie magazines." As Trevor looked at each picture, he had a rush of excitement such as he had seldom experienced. His mind continued to put those pictures back in his brain for weeks. He daydreamed about the pictures often at school, and a few weeks later, he stole one of those kinds of magazines from a local market. Trevor's zeal for pornography continued throughout junior high and high school. His language was a little coarse, he had been involved sexually with a couple of girls, and yet he still remained active in his youth group. He told me later, "I felt like I was living a double life. I wanted to be a good Christian. My quiet secret was that hardly a week went by without me viewing something pornographic."

What started as a semi-innocent viewing of porn with his friend and quick looks at *Playboy* magazines turned into a craving for bizarre sexual pornography he found on the Internet. He moved from what is called "soft-core" pornography to "hard-core" pornography. What finally scared him was the realization that he actually got sort of a "high" from watching child pornography (which is when children are engaged in sexual activity with adults or other children).

On the outside, Trevor looked like a regular Christian guy. On the inside, he was living a dual life. Trevor finally concluded that he needed help. Today, with the aid of a counselor, his family, friends, and God, he is breaking the strong addiction of pornography.

Is Trevor's story that unusual? No, I'm afraid not:

- Ninety-nine out of every one hundred guys have looked at pornographic materials.
- Nine out of ten girls answer yes when asked if they've viewed pornography.

Some studies tell us that 50 percent of the American teenage population views something pornographic each and every month. Wow! If you are not careful, pornography can get a hold of you very seductively and not let your mind forget the pictures you have placed there.

It's a fact that most people are drawn by curiosity to seek out a pornographic Web site or magazine or movie. Yet just because a person has viewed porn or read a dirty magazine or seen a dirty movie doesn't make him or her a pervert. Continued and constant obsession with pornographic material, however, is extremely dangerous. Unfortunately, the rapid growth of the Internet has made pornography more and more accessible to everyone, even those who aren't necessarily looking for it!

When speaking on the subject of torture, sexual perversion, and murders, a former police inspector said there had not been a sex murder in the history of the department in which the killer was not an avid viewer of pornography.

Pornography is a cheap substitute for sexuality as God created it to be. It often treats a human as a sex object. Pornography makes people feel dirty and uneasy about their sexuality. Sex is a gift from God. Sexuality is definitely not the perverted and often quite obscene thing it is portrayed as in so many books, magazines, and videos.

The Effects of Pornography

Many students have gone far deeper into pornography than they ever imagined they would. Some people haven't actually realized how negative the effects of their bad habits really are. Authorities give us several negative results of viewing pornographic material. I want to key in on two of the most common effects for teenagers.

A Warped View of Sexuality

People who frequently look at pornography begin to view sex as nothing but lust. Every element of love is replaced with a degrading and harmful view of sexuality. Far too often, in the words of Dr. Jerry Kirk, "Pornography exploits and dehumanizes women and children as discardable tools for the satisfaction of male lust, and children are abused mentally, emotionally, physically and spiritually to satisfy the hedonistic urges of pedophiles (child molesters). Women and children, when molested and cast aside, are left with indelible scars for the rest of their lives."[1]

People involved in pornography begin to tolerate and trivialize ungodly sexual behavior. I believe it is absolutely impossible to put a steady diet of pornography into your mind and expect to have a healthy Christian view of sexuality. Exposure to pornography makes people much more likely to believe that the greatest sexual joy comes *without* the commitment of marriage.

Guilt and Shame

When Trevor talked to me about his obsession with pornography, he was filled with the emotions of intense guilt and shame. He was beginning to isolate himself and draw away from his family, church, and friends. I'm convinced if Trevor would have continued much longer in his lifestyle and addiction to pornography, he would no longer have felt guilty. The Bible says that eventually these people, "having lost all sensitivity," will give themselves over "to sensuality so as to indulge in every kind of impurity, with a continual lust for more" (Ephesians 4:19).

Let's get something straight. Pornography is very dangerous. We cannot take this subject lightly. The power of a pornographic picture is all-consuming. Dr. Jerry Kirk gives us several important facts about pornography:

1. Pornography destroys the image of God in people. After all, we are created in God's image.
2. Pornography is addictive. "Pornography subtly winds around its users an ever-tightening chain of bondage."
3. Pornography is not Christ-honoring. Pornography openly mocks the most precious Christian beliefs. It belittles issues such as marital fidelity, morality, and commitment to Christ. Here's what the Scripture says, "Do not be deceived: Neither the sexually immoral nor idolaters . . . will inherit the kingdom of God. . . .

The body is not meant for sexual immorality, but for the Lord, and the Lord for the body" (1 Corinthians 6:9–10, 13).

4. Pornography is anti-sex. "Pornography promotes physical satisfaction without caring love, sex without responsibility, union without obligation for the consequences and exercise of the mating privilege with no regard to the immediate personal and physical consequences or the eternal consequences originally designated by God to accompany it."[2]

If you have been experimenting with pornography, I hope this chapter has sobered you to the facts and consequences of this lifestyle. Today is the day to stop the habit of viewing pornography. Similar to a recovering alcoholic who is unable to take even a sip of wine without going back to a life of alcoholism, you must decide to stop all behavior centered around pornography. Note the following steps:

Step One: *Today, make a commitment to God to never view another Web site, raunchy magazine, or movie again.*

Ask God to clean these memories from your mind and create a clean heart. The good news is that God is more powerful than pornography. He can and will forgive you of your sins and cleanse you from unrighteousness (see 1 John 1:9).

Step Two: *If you have talked to God and still feel drawn toward this addictive habit, seek help immediately.*

You are not alone. Thousands of well-meaning people in this world are addicted to pornography. Seek out a pastor, counselor, or trusted friend who will listen to you and help you develop a plan to overcome this chain of bondage around your life. Trevor needed to talk to a trusted

Christian counselor. That counselor is helping him learn to live one day at a time and remove any perverted sexuality from his life. With the help of God and his counselor, Trevor will overcome this obstacle.

Step Three: *Feed your mind good things.*

When we talk about pornography, we must talk about our minds. I like to use the old phrase "garbage in, garbage out." The principle is simple: If you put garbage into your mind, eventually garbage comes out. The more garbage you put into your mind, the more garbage there is to come out, in the form of all kinds of negative behavior. The best way to keep away from a negative thought life and negative behavior is to deprive your mind of garbage. Feed your mind good things—and good things will come out. Feed your mind trash— and guess what comes out? Paul offers some good advice about our thought lives: "Finally, brothers, whatever is true, whatever is noble, whatever is right, whatever is pure, whatever is lovely, whatever is admirable—if anything is excellent or praiseworthy—*think* about such things" (Philippians 4:8, emphasis added).

Dr. James Dobson calls the battle against pornography "the winnable war." The war can be won when we guard our hearts and minds by not allowing pornography to enter into our lives. Please do not underestimate the power of pornography. Run from it and run toward the love of God. He is the creator of positive, healthy sexuality. Everything else is a counterfeit.

Things to Think About

1. Given the strong message of this chapter, what are your reactions?

2. What do you think about the statement that pornography can be addictive?

3. Why do you suppose our culture allows such blatant pornographic material to reach the hands, eyes, and minds of young people so easily?

4. What are practical ways to keep away from pornography?

Respect Builders

1. Your mind matters. Read Philippians 4:8. Below, list the various kinds of things it suggests you think about—whatever is true, noble, and so on. Then, beside each of those words, write one or more things that fit into that category. The first two are done as an example for you. Fill in more of your own ideas for those two and then continue with the remaining words. Discuss your findings with your group or family.

Think about such things that are . . .	Things that fit the category
True	God's Word is true.
Noble	My grandparents are noble people.

Think about such things that are . . .	Things that fit the category

2. Search the Scriptures for thoughts on pornography. Read each verse or passage and then put in your own words how this section of Scripture might relate to pornography.

1 Corinthians 6:9–13	
Ephesians 4:18–19	
Ephesians 5:11	
Colossians 3:5–14	
Philippians 4:8	

Chapter Twenty-Three

Sexual Abuse

The following question was handed to me recently while I was speaking to a group of junior-high and senior-high students: "After someone has been sexually abused and hasn't told anyone about it and it has gone on for about five years, how can I try to forget and deal with it?" I receive such questions all the time. I never like to hear these questions. Yet after many years of experience, I now realize some important issues need to be thought about and questions need to be answered about sexual abuse. Did you know that at least:

- One out of three young women will be sexually abused by age eighteen
- One out of seven young men will be sexually abused by age eighteen

Diana was twelve when she told me that her grandfather had been "messing around" with her since she was five years old. Diana and her sisters had all been sexually abused by their grandfather.

Steve is thirty-one, but he still vividly remembers the exact evening a baby-sitter molested him. He was only eight years old.

Cassie had never been more excited. Matt finally asked her out on a date. She had dreamed of this night for almost two years. They got something to eat at a local diner and then went on to a house party. Matt and Cassie started drinking some beer from the keg in the backyard. Both were feeling pretty good from the alcohol buzz when Matt said, "Let's go upstairs." They found an empty room and started kissing. Matt's hands began to wander. Cassie felt uncomfortable, but didn't say anything. They were going too far. She was extremely nervous and very frightened. She said, "Stop!" He kept on going. Cassie tried to get away. Matt got forceful with her; Cassie cried and screamed. Cassie's dream night turned into a date rape.

These are not pretty stories. These are not happy statistics. Unfortunately, the statistics have names and faces. These people are friends I know, but I guarantee that you also know people who have struggled with the trauma of sexual abuse. You too may be a person who has been victimized by this tragedy we call "abuse."

Most people want to forget about this horrible experience. They pray it will go away, but it doesn't. When someone has been sexually abused, that person's pain tends to run deep and affects every aspect of life.

Here's what I generally tell students who have been abused:

1. *It's not your fault.* It's always the fault of the abuser. Sexual abuse is a horrible crime against you. The abuser is sick. If you blame yourself, you will get sick also.

2. *Seek help. Don't suffer in silence.* Most people who have been abused sexually are afraid to tell anyone. However, you can't get better without help. Your pain won't go away by itself. You can't simply wish it away. I urge people who have been abused

to not wait another day but to seek help immediately. If you wait, it only gets more difficult. It doesn't get easier.

3. *There is hope!* Unfortunately, millions have been abused. Many people have sought help and they have worked through their pain and are now living happy lives. Many people who have been abused believe that life will never be happy again. I can understand their emotions are paralyzed; however, the truth is that there is hope.

4. *God cares!* Frankly, most people who have experienced any kind of sexual abuse struggle in their relationships with God. I can understand their hurts and confusion. But I'm afraid too many people spend their energy blaming God instead of being comforted by Him. God wants to walk with you through the valley of hurt and disappointment. God weeps at your tragedy. He loves you and wants to heal your wounds.

This is a difficult chapter to write, and I struggle with the idea of including it. It seems, however, that no one is exempt from the harsh reality that tragic experiences happen to both good and bad people. If you or a friend of yours has faced some of the difficult experiences mentioned in the next few pages, seek outside help. This chapter does not provide all-inclusive information. It is written as an overview and a catalyst for action.

Date Rape

Date rape is a rape by someone you know or are dating. Frankly, most women who are raped are raped by someone they know and trust. Familiarity is enough to make them let down their guard, sometimes enough to make them wonder afterward whether they were really raped. A major myth about rape is that rapists are always strangers. Most rapes are committed by acquaintances. In fact, 75 to 80 percent of all teenage rapes are acquaintance or date rapes. If you have been date raped, immediately talk to someone who can help you. Although a date rape may not always result in a serious physical injury, it almost always causes severe emotional distress. You can receive help when you talk with a trusted counselor, pastor, or teacher.

Rape

As much as we all wish our society was always safe, it's not. Today, as never before, we must take precautions to prevent violent rape.

Rape is perhaps the ultimate outrage. Rape is one of the most horrible crimes committed against a person. Rape is most often inflicted not as a *sexual* crime, but as a *violent* crime. Most rapists are not so much interested in sexual pleasure as in hurting and frightening the victim. There is usually a great deal of anger, aggression, and hatred within the psychological makeup of the rapist. The vast majority of rape victims are women and girls, although a number of homosexual rapes of men and boys also occur each year. In this chapter, for convenience, I will refer to rape victims as women.

A person who has been raped should immediately call the police or go to a nearby hospital or rape crisis center. She will meet understanding people and be checked for injuries. The victim should not wash up before going to the hospital or center. A doctor will check for and collect evidence of the rape. Almost all the people, from doctors and nurses to police officers, are caring individuals who will compassionately help the rape victim through her initial shock and pain.

A rape victim should not go through this process alone. She should get the best medical treatment available along with some professional counseling. Receiving help from many trained individuals can and will make recovery from this painful experience a little easier.

Even better than coping with rape is preventing it. The very best protection is to stay away from potentially dangerous situations. Too many people have not thought through their actions and have lived to regret it. Here are a few suggestions to help prevent a rape. I encourage you to get in touch with your local rape prevention or crisis center for more information.

1. Never hitchhike. You're asking for trouble.
2. Don't walk or jog alone at night. This can be dangerous.
3. Carry a whistle, personal alarm, and/or pepper spray. There are a variety of such products that can be kept on your key chain so that they are readily on hand when you are alone.
4. Don't go out alone with a person you don't know. Too many people have been "picked up" at a dance, amusement park, or other public place without realizing they were being picked up by a rapist.
5. Don't flirt with someone you don't know. You could be flirting with a rapist.
6. Trust your instincts. If a friend or acquaintance has recently been making you feel nervous and uncomfortable, tell someone you can trust. It's better to be overly cautious than pretend like nothing bad could happen.

Here are some important facts about rape:

1. In the United States, a rape occurs once every two minutes.
2. Rape is one of the most frequent violent crimes, and its incidence is steadily increasing.

3. Victims range in age from young children to the elderly. They come from all lifestyles and socioeconomic groups.
4. Rape is a crime of violence. The rapist uses force or threats of harm to overpower and control the victim.
5. Although rape may or may not result in serious physical injuries, it always causes severe emotional distress.[1]

Incest

Incest is having sexual relations with a member of your own family, and sadly, incest is far more common than most people imagine. The most common form of incest is a father- or stepfather-daughter relationship, but many cases are reported each year of sexual relations between mother and son or brother and sister as well as between other relatives.

Incest is a serious and sensitive subject because it deals with family members. There is no such thing as a positive experience involving incest. An incestuous relationship must be stopped. If you or someone you know has been involved with incest, do not keep it to yourself. Report it to a proper authority immediately. A good place to start would be a minister, social worker, counselor, or police officer. The victim of incest will need help, and so will the aggressor. Sometimes victims of incest believe the abuse is their own fault. Such faulty thought patterns produce extreme and completely unnecessary guilt and self-blame. The victim of incest is not at fault and should not take the blame for someone else's sickness. Furthermore, no one is doing the aggressor a favor by keeping quiet about the problem.

At age sixteen, Alexis confided in me that she had been forced into an incestuous relationship with her father from the time she was seven until she was thirteen. I never would have guessed her problem in a million years. On the outside, she appeared to have it all together, but on the inside, she lived with tremendous amounts of hurt, anger, bitterness, and guilt. By the time she saw me, she was a volcano ready to explode at any minute.

Here are the steps I went through with Alexis. First, as her youth pastor, it was important for me to support and encourage her. She needed someone to lean on, so my wife and I both became good listeners for her. Second, we felt she needed extensive counseling, so we referred her to an experienced counselor and trusted friend. We let him deal with the major psychological trauma, and we continued as supportive friends and pastors. The Christian counselor reported the crime of incest to the county, and the family was able to go through intensive counseling. To this day Alexis still has her struggles and questions. But she has found an incredible amount of healing because she was willing to get the help she needed. Today Alexis is happily married and has a family of her own.

There *is* hope—just ask Alexis.

Things to Think About

1. Why do you suppose the statistics for sexual abuse are getting higher and higher?
2. To whom would you go if you were abused in any way?
3. Why are people afraid to tell anyone about their abuse?
4. What role should God play in the life of a person who has been abused?

Respect Builders

1. If a friend has been sexually abused, assist that person in seeking help immediately. The person needs professional care. You can be the catalyst for a positive life-changing decision.

2. Become aware of some of the signs of sexual abuse. Your friends may express their pain through behavior rather than words. The following is a list of several signals of sexual abuse, although the mere fact that a teenager has one or more of these behaviors does not always mean he or she has been sexually abused.

   a. Learning problems in school;
   b. Poor peer relationships;
   c. Self-destructive behavior, suicidal tendencies, frequent drug and alcohol abuse;
   d. Hostility and lack of trust toward adults;
   e. Major problems with authority figures;
   f. Seductive, promiscuous behavior;
   g. Running away;
   h. Fear of going home, fear of being left alone with the abuser;
   i. Severe depression;
   j. Pain, itching, bleeding, and bruises in the genital areas;
   k. Extremely low self-image.

   If you suspect an incestuous relationship, watch for these potential signals of abusive sexual behavior on the part of adults:
   a. Demands isolation of the child—discourages friendships, school activities, and dates;

b. Enforces restrictive control—allows few social events (actually extremely jealous);

c. Displays overdependence—sometimes the parent will depend on the child to fill needs usually met by the spouse or other adult;

d. Indulges in frequent drinking.[2]

Team Effort

A Case Study: Sexual Harassment and Abuse

Heather was baby-sitting at her ex-boyfriend Tom's house. She was close to his little sister and his family although she and Tom had broken up. Tom's stepfather had always been nice to Heather. In fact, she often wished she had a father as special as Tom's stepfather.

Tom's family was going out to dinner and a movie while Heather watched the youngest child. Tom's stepfather, Ted, would be home, but he would be working in the back room.

The moment Heather put the little girl to bed, Ted came into the kitchen and asked Heather if she wanted some popcorn. She loved popcorn and said, "Thanks, I can eat it while I'm watching this TV show." Ted made the popcorn and then sat down on the couch next to Heather and started watching the program with her. Heather complained about a sore back she had gotten from playing softball. So he began to rub her back. At first he rubbed outside her sweater, but after a while moved his hands under her sweater.

Heather froze. She didn't know what to do. She didn't know if this nice man was going to go further or if he was just doing an innocent favor. Heather was tense and nervous. In a soft voice, he told her to relax; it would be better for her backache.

The phone rang. Heather was grateful for the distraction. Ted, reluctantly it seemed, got up to answer the phone.

1. If you were Heather, what would you do?
2. Do you think it was okay to baby-sit while the stepfather was still home? Why or why not?
3. If you were Heather's youth pastor and she told you this story, what would you say or do?
4. If you were Heather, would you tell Tom or his mother about this incident? Why or why not?

Epilogue

Thanks so much for investing the time to read this book. I have never met a person who has regretted accepting nothing less than God's standards for sexuality in relationships. I meet people almost every day who *do* regret past unwise decisions about their sexuality. Basically, it's a matter of commitment to the spiritual discipline of being sexually pure and having sexual integrity; the spiritual discipline is even more important sometimes than the physical discipline. The people I see making right decisions about their sexuality are people who have included God in the process. Remember, He created sex and He wants the best for you.

Along the way to accepting nothing less than God's best, it will take a commitment to the Purity Code (see chapter four). The Purity Code is:

In honor of God, my family, and my future spouse, I commit my life to sexual purity.

This involves:

- Honoring God with your **body**

  "The body is not meant for sexual immorality, but for the Lord, and the Lord for the body" (1 Corinthians 6:13).

- Renewing your **mind** for the good

  "Do not conform any longer to the pattern of this world, but be transformed by the renewing of your mind. Then you will be able to test and approve what God's will is—his good, pleasing and perfect will" (Romans 12:2).

- Turning your **eyes** from worthless things

  "Your eye is a lamp that provides light for your body. When your eye is good, your whole body is filled with light" (Matthew 6:22 NLT).

- Guarding your **heart** above all else

  "Guard your heart above all else, for it determines the course of your life" (Proverbs 4:23 NLT).

Signature: _____ Date: _____

My challenge to you today is to make a commitment to the Purity Code. I am looking for one million courageous young people who refuse to settle for anything less than God's best by committing to the Purity Code. I hope you will join me in this incredible journey toward health and wholeness.

Notes

Chapter Two: How Far Is Too Far?

1. Larry Richards, *How Far Can I Go?* (Grand Rapids: Zondervan Publishing House, 1979), 96.

2. Ibid.

Chapter Three: Why Wait?

1. C. S. Lewis, *The Screwtape Letters* (New York: Macmillan, Inc., 1982), 83.

2. Ray E. Short, *Sex, Love, or Infatuation: How Can I Really Know?* (Minneapolis: Augsburg Publishing House, 1990), 83.

3. Ibid., 83, 88–89.

4. Larry Richards, *How Far Can I Go?*, 43.

Chapter Four: The Purity Code

1. Dr. James Dobson, *Focus on the Family* magazine (April 1990).

Chapter Ten: Peer Pressure

1. Aaron Haas, *Teenager Sexuality: A Survey of Teenage Sexual Behavior* (Los Angeles: Pinnacle Books, 1981), 46–49.

2. Ibid.

Chapter Fourteen: Drugs and Drinking

1. For a more in-depth look at this subject, you may want to see Steve Arterburn

and Jim Burns, *How to Talk to Your Kids About Drugs* (Eugene, OR: Harvest House, 2007).

2. Ibid.

Chapter Fifteen: Guilt and Forgiveness

1. James Dobson, *Emotions: Can You Trust Them?* (Ventura, CA: Gospel Light, 1980), 18.

Chapter Sixteen: Options for the Pregnant

1. www.physiciansforlife.org/content/view/825/2/

2. www.webmd.com/baby/guide/pregnancy-tests; www.revolutionhealth.com/conditions/reproductive-health/infertility/prevention/home-test

3. Charlie Shedd, *The Stork Is Dead* (Dallas: Word Inc., 1968), 61–63.

Chapter Seventeen: What About Abortion?

1. Focus on the Family, *The First Nine Months* (New York: Dell Publishing Co., Inc., 1990), 3.

Chapter Eighteen: Masturbation

1. David Wilkerson, *This Is Loving?* (Ventura, CA: Gospel Light, 1972), 40.

2. Charlie Shedd, *The Stork Is Dead*, 72.

Chapter Twenty: Sexually Transmitted Diseases (STDs)

1. Arvis J. Olsen, *Sexuality: Guidelines for Teenagers* (Grand Rapids: Baker Book House, 1981), 63–64.

Chapter Twenty-One: Homosexuality

1. Tim Stafford, *A Love Story: Questions and Answers on Sex* (Grand Rapids: Zondervan, 1977), 103.

Chapter Twenty-Two: Pornography

1. Dr. Jerry R. Kirk, *What the Bible Says: Ten Reasons Why You Should Get Involved in the Fight Against Pornography* (Colorado Springs: Focus on the Family, 1989), 5.

2. Ibid.

Chapter Twenty-Three: Sexual Abuse

1. Jim Burns, *Uncommon Youth Ministry* (Ventura, CA: Gospel Light, 2008).

2. Ibid.

More From Jim Burns

Jim Burns, president of HomeWord, lays a positive foundation for parenting with practical strategies and illustrations, teaching how to create a warm, grace-filled home.

Confident Parenting

Small Group/Church DVD Package also available

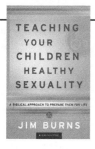

Trusted family authority provides a simple and practical guide for parents to help their children develop a healthy perspective regarding their bodies and sexuality.

Teaching Your Children Healthy Sexuality

Parent/Child Combo Pack with Audio Resource also available

Tackles the tough and sensitive issues in sexuality to prepare preteens for their adolescent years, instilling godly values about sex, their body, and relationships.

The Purity Code

The Purity Code: Audio Resource also available

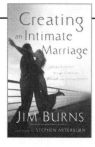

The host of *HomeWord* shows couples how to set the emotional thermostat for a more satisfying marriage filled with affection, warmth, and encouragement.

Creating an Intimate Marriage

Small Group/Church DVD Package also available

Parent and Family Resources from HomeWord

Parenting Teenagers for Positive Results

This popular resource is designed for small groups and Sunday schools. The kit includes a DVD to begin each of the six sessions featuring a real family situation played out in humorous family vignettes followed by words of wisdom by youth and family expert, Jim Burns, Ph.D., from HomeWord. Each DVD session averages 5 minutes.

The kit contains:
DVD, CD with printable leader's guides and participant guides.

Creating an Intimate Marriage

Jim Burns wants every couple to experience a marriage filled with A.W.E.: affection, warmth, and encouragement. He shows husbands and wives how to make their marriage their priority as they discover ways to repair the past, communicate and resolve conflict, refresh their marriage spiritually, and more!

Confident Parenting

This is a must-have resource for today's family. Let Jim Burns help you to tackle overcrowded lives, negative family patterns, while creating a grace-filled home and raising kids who love God and themselves.

How to Talk to Your Kids About Drugs

Kids can't avoid being exposed to drug use today, some as early as grade school. Packed with practical information and time-proven prevention techniques, this book is a realistic, up-to-date, comprehensive plan for drug-proofing your kids. And if you suspect your kids are already using drugs and alcohol, respected counselor Steve Arterburn and well-known parenting and family expert Jim Burns offer step-by-step advice to get them straight and sober.

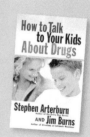

Tons of helpful resources for parents and youth.
Visit our online store at www.HomeWord.com
Or call us at 800-397-9725

HOME WORD

WHERE PARENTS GET REAL ANSWERS

Get Equipped with HomeWord...

LISTEN
HomeWord Radio
programs reach over 800 communities nationwide with *HomeWord with Jim Burns* – a daily ½ hour interview feature, *HomeWord Snapshots* – a daily 1 minute family drama, and *HomeWord this Week* – a ½ hour weekend edition of the daily program, and our one-hour program.

CLICK
HomeWord.com
provides advice and resources to millions of visitors each year. A truly interactive website, HomeWord.com provides access to parent newsletter, Q&As, online broadcasts, tip sheets, our online store and more.

READ
HomeWord Resources
parent newsletters, equip families and Churches worldwide with practical Q&As, online broadcasts, tip sheets, our online store and more. Many of these resources are also packaged digitally to meet the needs of today's busy parents.

ATTEND
HomeWord Events
Understanding Your Teenager, Building Healthy Morals & Values, Generation 2 Generation and Refreshing Your Marriage are held in over 100 communities nationwide each year. HomeWord events educate and encourage parents while providing answers to life's most pressing parenting and family questions.

A Ministry with *Jim Burns*

In response to the overwhelming needs of parents and families, Jim Burns founded HomeWord in 1985. HomeWord, a Christian organization, equips and encourages parents, families, and churches worldwide.

Find Out More
Sign up for our FREE daily
e-devotional and parent e-newsletter
at HomeWord.com, or call 800.397.9725.

HomeWord.com